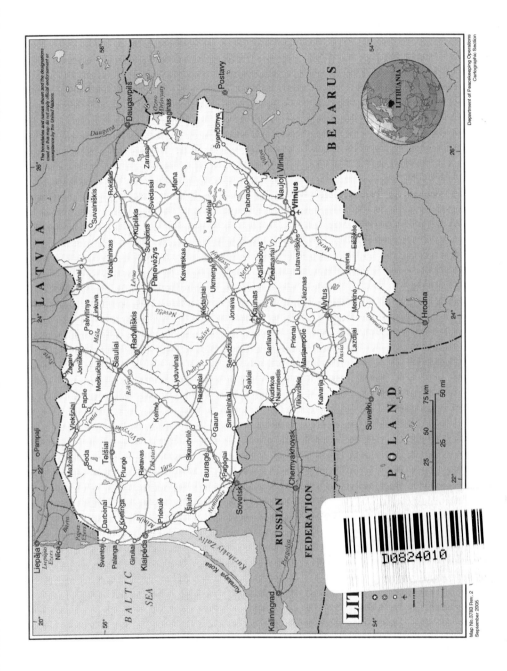

LATVIA

BELARUS

LITHUANIA

POLAND

RUSSIAN
FEDERATION

BALTIC
SEA

Department of Peacekeeping Operations
Cartographic Section

Map No. 3769 Rev. 2
September 2005

D0824010

0   25   50   75 km
0   25   50 mi

Second Edition, 2015

On the cover:
Recent arrivals: the Baranauskas family in Brockton, MA, winter 1949–50.

Lithuanian Roots in American Soil:
A Memoir of the Barūnas Family

Audronė Barūnas Willeke
Text and Translation

and

Danutė Barūnas
Graphic Design

"I slept and dreamt that life was joy.
I awoke and saw that life was service.
I acted and behold, service was joy."

– Rabindranath Tagore (1861–1941)
Bengali author,
Nobel Prize in Literature, 1913

Quote taken from a notebook of aphorisms that Kazys Barūnas
collected. These were various reflections, by writers and
philosophers from around the world, on how to live a good life.

Table of Contents

Preface

This family history was initiated by a question from our niece, Kristina (Kris) Barūnas Jepsen. She told me one day that she was curious about the memoir her grandfather, Kazys Barūnas, had written, a copy of which she inherited from her father Rimvydas. However, the memoir was in Lithuanian, and though she had learned some Lithuanian as a girl, she did not know enough to read this book. "I need to find someone who will translate this for me," she said. "Do you know someone who can do that?" she asked. I knew immediately who this "someone" had to be. "Yes, I said, "I'm the one who has to do it, for it will require more than just translation." Kris is an avid collector of family stories; she compiled a family tree, and, a media specialist by profession, she has created wonderful slide shows of special events from old photographs and films. She wants to pass on this information and history to her two children, Katherine and Donald.

It seemed to me that a history of the family in English would be useful not only to her and her family, but also to my brother Algis' children Laura and Alex, and to our son Vytas and his wife Claire. These young people knew and loved their Lithuanian grandparents, whom they called Tėvukas (grandfather) and Močiutė (grandmother). A family history could be a source of information and inspiration for them and perhaps for future generations. Our family friends and other readers may find this family memoir interesting as well, for it tells a rather dramatic story of one family's survival during World War II. It relates the typical fate of war refugees from Lithuania who found shelter and a new life in the United States.

With such a project in mind, I conferred with my sister Danutė (Dana), who is a graphic design specialist, with the skills to turn an ordinary manuscript into an illustrated book. We agreed to work as a team on this endeavor. In reading the manuscript, Dana has provided invaluable corrections and additional information. This book is the product of our joint labor. It is a tribute of love and respect that we pay to our parents, each an amazing individual in his/her own way.

I'd like to acknowledge the support of my husband, Klaus Willeke, who read the first draft with great care and provided useful suggestions. Thanks also to brother Algis for his helpful comments on the manuscript.

Audronė (Audra) Barūnas Willeke   Danutė (Dana) Barūnas
Orinda, California   Pembroke, Massachusetts

September, 2014

Introduction

W hat makes us a family? Certainly, we share a common gene pool that shows up in some physical similarities. Since we think we look so different, my sister Danutė (Dana) and I are surprised when people immediately recognize us as sisters and comment, "There's a lot of resemblance." But equally important, we are a family because we share experiences that extend over our entire lifetimes, from childhood to old age. We share family stories that have been passed down orally and that help to shape our identities. Since the story of our family has taken place on two continents and much of the material is preserved in the Lithuanian language, Dana and I have decided to prepare this memoir in English in order to make it available to the generations who now live in the United States and who have no access to the Lithuanian language and not much contact with their relatives in Lithuania. Sooner or later, most people wish to know something about their ancestors: Who were they? Where did they come from? What sort of people were they? What kind of lives did they lead? In our case also: how and why did the Barūnas family leave Lithuania and settle in the United States?

Three years after arriving in the United States, in 1952, our father, Kazys Barūnas, began to write his memoirs. I remember seeing him bent over his desk in his study in Savin Hill (a neighborhood in Boston), filling small notebooks with his clear and precise handwriting. The family history that he compiled was done completely from memory, since he had no documents to aid him. With the precision of the engineer that he was by profession, he sketched out a map of the village where he had grown up, including the homesteads of all the families who lived there. Our father had an excellent memory, thus his recall of names and dates was amazingly accurate. Even as a young girl, watching him at work on this memoir, I knew that the force driving him to write was his great homesickness for his country, Lithuania. While living in a culture and language that felt strange and alien to him, he could transport himself in memories back to his native land.

Father wrote about his and our mother's family origins, how they met, how they survived the Soviet occupation and fled to Germany, how they lived in displaced person camps, and how they came to the United States. Once he reached the United States in his narrative, he lost interest in continuing the memoir. Years later, at my urging, he resumed his writing to give a brief account of our life in this country, ending in 1988. I then typed his memoir on computer and had it bound, presenting the finished book to him in honor of his 76th birthday, with copies for all my siblings.

Father's memoir is an important source for Dana and me as we prepare this expanded family history. However, this is not just a translation of his words into English. Father explained his interpretations of world events, he commented extensively on the politics of the time. On the other hand, he paid less attention to what may have seemed to him the insignificant events and struggles that made up our personal lives. Dana and I want to include these personal stories, passed on orally, or in letters, or stored in our memories.

The story of how our family came to America is fairly typical for World War II refugees. However, you will find here a unique set of characters and unexpected twists of fate. Many families have a skeleton or two in the closet and ours does as well. While our father discreetly avoided mention of embarrassing or scandalous events and individuals, this family history will try to give a fuller picture of the past to the extent that we know it. We believe the next generations will find our story compelling and worth reading.

Our last name needs explanation. Our father's family was Baranauskas, a name of Slavic origin deriving from the word "baran" which means "sheep." The name has a variety of spellings in different East European languages. For example, in Polish the name appears as Baranowski; from Cyrillic Russian it is transliterated as Baranovski or Baranovsky. Since the endings of Lithuanian last names change depending on whether the name refers to a man, a married woman, or an unmarried daughter, we arrived in the United States with the following names: our father was Kazimieras (Kazys) Baranauskas, our mother Jadvyga (Jadzė) Baranauskienė, the daughters Audronė (Audra) Baranauskaitė, Danutė (Dana) Baranauskaitė, and the sons Rimvydas (Rimas) Baranauskas and Algis (Al) Baranauskas. I was often frustrated during penmanship practice in grammar school as I tried to fit my enormously long name, Audronė Baranauskas, on one line. Relief came when the entire family became US citizens in 1955 and shortened our last name to Barūnas. Our father had a special reason for the change, besides convenience: he felt that Barūnas was more Lithuanian than the original name of Slavic origin.

You will notice that we have used two different fonts in this book. The passages translated from our father's memoir are in italics. Passages in which I summarize the content of our father's writing in my own words or those sections written by me are in ordinary typeface.

Here are some tips on the pronunciation of special Lithuanian letters in names of people and places:

ė   broad e like in ch**air**

č   **ch**ur**ch**

š   **sh**oe

ž . plea**s**ure

ū   long u like f**oo**d

j   like **ya**

y   long e like in s**ee**d

The final e at the end of a word is always pronounced.

Chapter 1: Crossing the Atlantic

I was holding on to my brother Rimvydas as best I could as the path rose up toward me like a steep hill. With my other hand I clutched the railing that ran the length of the long corridor. I panted as I pulled my brother along behind me. He swayed back and forth on his short legs, struggling to keep his balance. Suddenly we both lurched forward — now the corridor was going down in a steep descent. Our mother was behind us, leading the two-year-old twins, Danutė and Algis in each hand. Our cabin seemed so far away. I wanted desperately to reach it, so I could lay down on my bunk where the motion of the boat seemed calmer and my stomach less likely to release its content. We were slowly making our way back from the dining room after another useless effort by our mother to feed us something. The corridor was thick with the smell of vomit left behind by people who did not reach a toilet in time. I tried to hold my breath, worried that the same embarrassing thing will happen to me. Mother had tried to get some milk for the twins — some days she succeeded, but today the dining room staff had not been sympathetic. There were younger babies on board and the ship's kitchen was running out of powdered milk. Food supplies were low because our crossing was taking much longer than planned. We were offered some oranges and surprisingly I was able to keep a bit down. The dining room had been rather empty again, since many of the passengers had stopped eating.

Our ship, the *USS General S.D. Sturgis*, had departed from Bremerhaven, Germany, on October 14, 1949, with about a thousand refugees bound for New York. The Atlantic Ocean was unusually stormy that fall. A ship with refugees traveling just ahead of us encountered some damage and radioed our captain with advice to take a detour from the usual route to avoid the full brunt of the hurricane-like winds. Instead of the expected six, our small ship tossed in the waves for twelve days. Even in the best of weather the crossing would have been a difficult one for our family. The Sturgis was no luxury cruiser, rather a troop transport that had been built in Richmond, California during World War II to ferry American soldiers to battlefields in the Pacific and in Europe. After the war, it was rebuilt to serve as transport for displaced persons.

Our cabin had four bunk beds. We children slept two to a bed, while our mother had the third. A woman we did not know occupied the fourth bunk bed with her baby. The men slept at the bottom level of the ship, in large rooms with dozens of bunks. During the day they labored on the boat, performing various maintenance chores as compensation for our passage. This was a free trip. Our mother had to care for us four by herself. Feeling sick and afraid, we stayed in our beds as much as possible, but she had to get up and do what was necessary to clean us up, clothe us, and try to get us to eat or at least drink a bit. Worst were the emergency drills that happened mostly at night. When the ear-splitting alarm sounded, mother woke us up, placed life vests on us, and struggled out with us to the appointed meeting place. Though we were told it was a drill, it frightened us to be woken up suddenly and taken out in the cold night into a crowd of people. The twins, crying quietly, didn't want to put on their life vests. The ocean looked so black and vast, our rocking, creaking ship so small.

In the evenings, we sometimes met our father on one of the decks where the men came to be reunited briefly with the women and children. Because of the waves that washed over the lower deck, we were not always allowed outdoors or only on the upper deck where the wind blew fiercest. This crossing of the Atlantic was so traumatic for our mother that for the rest of her life she refused to set foot in a boat.

As we approached the shores of North America the winds died down and the sea calmed. I remember our last night on board. The refugees were too excited to stay in their cabins. They gathered on the upper deck in small groups, by nationality. There were Lithuanians, Latvians, Estonians, Poles, Ukrainians, and others who had fled their homelands when the Soviet army invaded. All these people were facing an unknown future in a new country. If our parents were worried, they did not let us know. We felt secure in their care. Our father had a small English grammar book that he had been using on the boat to learn some English. I knew that I had to learn a new language. A boy, slightly older than I, told me that once we get off the ship in America, no one will understand Lithuanian or even German. I was baffled when he told me that in English the

word "nine" does not mean the same as German "nein." I thought to myself, "English is a silly language — I don't want to learn it."

How and why did the Baranauskas family — father Kazys (age 37), mother Jadvyga (age 27), five-year-old Audronė, four-year-old Rimvydas, and the two-year-old twins Danutė and Algis — come to be on this boat heading for America? What strange twists of fate brought us here, while the rest of our relatives remained behind in Lithuania? The story of this journey is worth remembering and passing on to you, the next generations born in the United States.

Chapter 2: Kazys' Origin

Birthplace

Our father, Kazys (officially Kazimieras, Casimir in English) Barūnas, was born on February 27, 1912 in Žaunieriškiai, a village located a few miles north of the town of Alytus in southwestern Lithuania, on the left bank of the Nemunas River. The meaning of the name is curious — it is of Polish origin and, according to our father, means "Warriors." A road heading north from Alytus passes through the center of this village and continues to the parish village of Rumbonys, then on to the forest of Punia. Although our father had no access to documents on the history of his home village, he wrote down what he knew from personal experience about it and similar Lithuanian villages.

Kazimieras Baranauskas at age 18.

In the past, Lithuanian farmers lived in small clusters of a dozen to twenty-something families, with their homesteads close to one another, usually on both sides of a road that was partly paved with stones in the vicinity of the village. The dwellings and granaries were usually built with the sides of the buildings toward the road. Flower gardens grew under the windows of the houses. Thus the village took on the look of a small town. The cottages were constructed of logs, the cracks filled with moss, and the steep roofs were covered with straw. The cottages were built directly on the ground or on low stone foundations. The floors were of beaten clay, the windows small. The barns, too, had floors of beaten clay on which the farmers thrashed the grain by hand with flails. These barns often had no windows at all or only very small ones.

All the land in the village was divided into three sections and each of these sections was subdivided into individual properties. Thus, the property of each farmer consisted of three fields, each one long and narrow, at a distance from one *another and from the homestead. In case of a fire, the entire village often burned down because the homesteads stood close together and modern firefighting equipment did not exist. Another disadvantage to this type of village structure was that conflicts frequently arose between neighbors because of damages done by domestic animals or because farmers encroached on each other's property. Clearly, modern farming methods were impossible under such conditions.*

The village of Žaunieriškiai belonged to the Province of Suvalkija that our father believed to be culturally more progressive than other regions of Lithuania because it bordered on Poland and was thus oriented toward the West. In the 19th century, czarist Russia ruled all of Lithuania and a part of Poland. The Lithuanian Suvalkija Province was administered together with czarist Poland. After the Napoleonic Wars, a new legal system was introduced here, the Napoleonic Code, and serfdom was abolished in 1807, whereas in the rest of Lithuania it lasted until 1861. Because of these advantages, Suvalkija was the first province in Lithuania to undertake agrarian reform by eliminating the old villages.

Kazys was not sure when the old village of Žaunieriškiai was split up into individual farms — he guessed it happened in the middle of the 19th century. In his youth, some remnants of the original village were still visible — part of a fruit orchard, an old shed, and an abandoned cemetery on a sandy hill. It was sad to pass by this ancient resting place, where

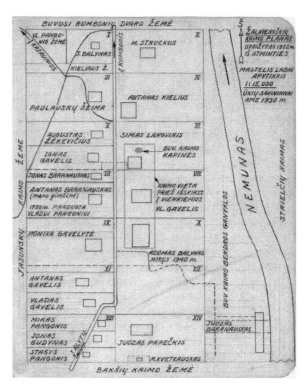

Plan of Žaunieriskiai drawn by Kazys.

farmers sometimes plowed up human bones. In our father's time, eleven farm families lived in the area of Žaunieriškiai, many of them related. The farms were small and all about the same size — by father's estimate his family owned 25 hectares or 62 acres. However, these farmers were skilled and industrious, their farms were well maintained and relatively prosperous. They were ambitious for their children and were among the first in the district to send some of them for vocational training and education beyond the elementary level. From this village, men of our father's generation studied for the priesthood and attended teachers' colleges. Several of them occupied high ranks in independent Lithuania's military: in aviation and in the cavalry.

In our father's time, the most famous person in the village, and highly respected in the whole district, was Adomas (Adam) Balynas. Father called him an "aristocrat of the spirit," an unusually enlightened individual. Balynas was born about 1885, studied at the Teachers' College in Veiveriai, taught at various schools, then, a few years before the start of World War I (1914), he returned to teach at an elementary school in a village near Žaunieriškiai. Many area youth had the good fortune to study in his school, which, like

other elementary schools of the time, was a one-room school with only three grades. However, this dedicated educator was able to give his pupils much more than just the basic skills in reading, writing, and arithmetic. Balynas also established evening classes in the village, where young people could continue to learn and to engage in cultural activities during the long winter evenings. After Lithuania regained independence in1918, some of Balynas' students filled responsible positions in government at the local and national levels with only an elementary school education. Kazys paid a moving tribute to this teacher:

Adomas Balynas

Adomas Balynas had the soul of an artist — he was a skilled musician and actor... He organized a good chorus and directed a theater group whose performances were of a higher quality than usual for amateur productions. Under his direction, I took my first steps on stage and soon was chosen to play the major roles. I also assisted him with organizing the theater productions. During World War I, Balynas' family had fled to Russia, along with many others. While there, he was able to see first-rate Russian plays and learned a lot about theater. Balynas was a skilled speaker who, with simple, sincere words was able to move his listeners, regardless of their age or education.... Toward the end of his life, Balynas wrote interesting memoirs and poetry. However, these writings seem to have remained unpublished. Adomas Balynas died early in 1940 and was buried in the cemetery at Rumbonys. I came to his funeral from Kaunas and spoke the last words of farewell.

Adomas Balynas became an important mentor to our father, one who influenced the further course of his life. Inspired by him, Kazys developed a love for theater and acting, for public speaking, and for writing poetry. After immigrating to the United States, in the Boston and Daytona Beach Lithuanian communities, he was much in demand as a speaker and reciter of poetry at various events. We, his children, remember his impressive acting in numerous plays, especially in his role as Marley's ghost in Charles Dickens' "A Christmas Carol." He had a prodigious memory and could recite long passages of Lithuanian poetry by heart, including poems memorized in elementary school.

Father's Family

Grandfather Jurgis (1838–1920)

The Baranauskas family name was quite common in the villages of the district. Kazys did not know when the first Baranauskas settled in Žaunieriškiai, but he was certain that his great-grandfather Mikolas (Michael), born early in the 19th century, already lived there. One of Mikolas' sons, Antanas (Anthony) married and settled in the village of Taučionys. Another son married into the village of Paliepiai, on the right bank of the Nemunas River. The family homestead in Žaunieriškiai came down to Jurgis (George), our father's grandfather. This grandfather was born in 1838, died in 1920, and was buried, along with other family members, in the cemetery of the parish village of Rumbonys, a few miles north of Žaunieriškiai. Since Kazys was already nine years old when his grandfather died, he remembered him quite well.

He was a sturdy, healthy man of average height. Though mild mannered, he was rather strict and determined in his behavior. He enjoyed drinking whiskey but was not an alcoholic. He liked to eat well and plenty. Though he didn't smoke, he sniffed tobacco. When he was in a good mood, he even gave us children some to sniff, causing us to sneeze wildly. He seldom laughed, was rather serious, hard working, and orderly. He was able to read and to sign his name (he signed "Baranauckas") but I don't know if he was able to write more than that. He prayed from a Polish prayer book, although he hardly knew how to speak Polish or Russian.

Grandfather Jurgis married Marija Marcinkevičiūtė from the village of Butrimiškiai who gave him three sons and five daughters. After she died (before 1900), he married a second time but didn't have any more children. The oldest of the three sons, our father's father Antanas (Anthony), inherited the homestead, another son, Jonas (John, 1879–1947), remained in Žaunieriškiai, while the third son, Adomas, emigrated to the United States. Four of the daughters, Morta (Martha), Ona (Ann), Marė, and Petronė, married farmers from nearby villages, but one of them, Emilija (Emily), who married a Jankauskas, emigrated to the United States. Kazys did not have any further information about the aunt and uncle who emigrated.

From the 1880s until the start of World War I in 1914, large numbers of young Lithuanians, like other East Europeans, emigrated to the industrial cities of Western Europe and to the United States to look for work. Statistics show that from 1899–1914 a total of 252,600 Lithuanians emigrated, about twice as many men as women. Because families had many children, the younger sons and daughters could not hope to inherit their parents' property. The small farms could only be passed down to one or two children. Lithuanian immigrants to the United States settled in and around cities like Boston, New York, and in smaller cities, such as Brockton and Worcester, where they found work in factories. Others traveled to Chicago to work in the stockyards where they formed the largest Lithuanian émigré community. Still others found work in the coalmines of Pennsylvania. While we don't know where Kazys' uncle Adomas (Adam) and aunt Emilija (Emily) settled in the United States, we can imagine the hard life they faced here.

Our father's aunts and uncles had large families, seven to nine children, except for Jonas, who had only three. Because his uncle Jonas had received training as a blacksmith, when grandfather Jurgis divided his property, he gave the homestead and major portion of land to his oldest son Antanas, our father's father, while Jonas, as craftsman, received only about 16 acres and some new farm buildings. It is clear from Kazys' memoir how much Lithuanians valued their land and how they clung to it. Having to leave their land or to sell it was a momentous and painful decision.

His grandfather Jurgis left a strong impression on young Kazys, who described at length this man's exceptional skill with horses.

My grandfather loved animals, above all, horses. He was renowned for his knowledge of horses. When neighbors were buying a horse, they would invite my grandfather as a horse expert to give his opinion. My grandfather's horses were famous in the whole district. Good horses at that time were expensive, so there was no lack of horse thieves. Gypsies were often involved in that activity. In order to safeguard his excellent horses, grandfather built the horse stable right next to the house. If something were to happen during the night, for instance, if a horse were to tumble over or a thief approach, grandfather would hear this. The story goes that grandfather was returning home one night from Alytus in his wagon, perhaps with some drinks under his belt, when two thieves jumped out of the ditch along the road. One tried to grab the reins of the horses to stop them, while the other leaped up on the wagon to attack grandfather. But grandfather smacked the whip on his horses and they took off like lightening, knocking down the first thief. Then grandfather managed to strike the second thief with his whip as well. The frightened horses dashed right by the house, so grandfather had to detour back. Even after my grandfather's time, we continued to have good horses on our farm. In those days, good horses were a farmer's pride, especially among the young men. To drive a wagon with fine horses gave them more pride then driving in a modern Cadillac today.

Kazys once told Dana that his grandfather's horses were so valuable that he installed a big metal bar across the stable doors to keep out thieves. Perhaps there's such a thing as a "horse gene" which skipped two generations to appear in full force in Jurgis' great-granddaughter Dana who discovered her affinity for horses as a young woman. She owned two horses and rode many more — horses became the "love of her life."

Father Antanas (1873–1940)

Kazys' father Antanas was born on January 1, 1873 in Žaunieriškiai and died almost 68 years of age on December 14, 1940. Like his father before him, he too is buried in the parish cemetery at Rumbonys.

Although his facial Father's two brothers Adomas and Vladas with their father, *features were different, my* Antanas Baranauskas. March 1922. *father resembled grand-father Jurgis in temperament and physique. Slow in manner and kind-hearted, he was fair and considerate, especially toward the neighbors. He liked to socialize and converse with people, but at home he was quiet. He carefully avoided quarrels. In his farming methods he was conservative, perhaps because he lacked*

the initiative to innovate and because he did not like to take risks. He was pious and enjoyed singing religious hymns. Having finished elementary school, he was fond of reading and read a lot. Because of his fair and conciliatory nature, he was respected by people in the district and was elected village elder in Žaunieriškiai for several years. Whatever responsibilities he had, he tried to complete them conscientiously. Around the year 1900 my father married Magdalena Kardišauskaitė with whom he lived faithfully and harmoniously all his life. Like in every marriage, occasional disagreements came up between them, especially due to the shortages they faced in raising a large family. But these disagreements always remained within the family.

Mother Magdalena
(1883–1965)

My mother Magdalena was born about 1883 in the village of Pošnia, in Miroslavas parish, in the district of Alytus. My mother's father, Jonas Kardišauskas, was a prosperous farmer. He was very hard working, maintaining his farm in a wise and exemplary fashion. He was quite well educated and for some time served as chief of the entire district. He liked to rub elbows with the upper classes and liked to show off with his ability to speak Polish, which at that time was a mark of distinction. He died in 1922 at about the age of 80. The Pošnia railroad station was later built on his land.

The family name of my mother's mother was Žilinskaitė; she was from the village of Sapatiškiai in Alytus district. My mother had six siblings: Ieva (Eve, 1868–1944) who

Father's mother, Magdalena Kardišauskaitė Baranauskienė.

emigrated to the United States and settled in Shenandoah, Pennsylvania; Jonas (1860–1946) who married a local woman and remained in the village of Pošnia; Baltrus (1870–1940) who inherited part of the farm; Juozas (1880–1962) who also inherited part of the farm; Petras (Peter) who emigrated to the United States, to Frackville, Pennsylvania.; and Morta (Martha) who married Antanas

Jaškevičius from the village of Kalesninkai, Odrija parish, district of Alytus. All these aunts and uncles had large families.

Kazys does not mention in his memoir the scandal concerning his Aunt Ieva who came to the United States, but he told us the story orally. It seems that Ieva, still unmarried, became pregnant and was faced with the embarrassment this would cause her and her family. Such situations were common enough and the usual solution was for the couple to marry. But Ieva either could not or would not marry the man involved. She kept her pregnancy a secret. Then one Sunday, remaining at home while the rest of the family went to church, Ieva took the cash that her father kept hidden and disappeared. With that money she found her way to Pennsylvania to look for her brother Petras who had settled there earlier. The parents were heart-broken when they returned home from church and saw what had happened. Presumably, Ieva had left them a letter. The father, especially, was devastated — Ieva was his oldest and his favorite child. In Pennsylvania, Ieva located her brother, now a coal miner, who took her in. After the birth of her son, John, she soon married another coal miner, a fellow Lithuanian. They settled in the large Lithuanian community of Shenandoah and had more children. As soon as she could, Ieva sent back to her father the money she had "borrowed." Some years after our family came to the United States, Kazys traced down these relatives and we drove from Boston to Pennsylvania to visit them. By then, his Aunt Ieva and Uncle Petras had died, but their families were very welcoming. Some of the family members had moved elsewhere: to Buffalo, NY, to Washington D. C., and to North Carolina. In later years, our family visited these people as well. My husband Klaus and I also stopped in Shenandoah in the 1970s and still found some of our father's relatives living there.

From the way he described his mother, it is clear that Kazys was very fond of her. In contrast to his quiet, slow-tempered father, his mother was lively and sociable. Our father may have inherited his eloquence, his way with words, from her.

My mother was short, very energetic, and industrious. She was cheerful, liked to talk and to socialize. She loved songs and sang well herself. She was also an excellent storyteller. My kind-hearted mother loved us children very much and sacrificed herself to provide for us. She died June 12, 1965 and was buried in the town cemetery of Veiveriai.

About 1955, more than ten years after they had fled from Lithuania, our parents received the first correspondence from the relatives they had left behind. Although still struggling hard themselves, they immediately began to send packages of clothing and food to their relatives. Our father was especially concerned to help his mother, by then a widow, who was living with Kazys' sister Monika in Veiveriai. I remember how moved our father was when he received the first photo of his mother.

The Siblings

Kazys' mother Magdalena gave birth to eleven children, all at the homestead in Žaunieriškiai. Three of them died as infants or young children, while eight reached adulthood. Our father grew up with five brothers and two sisters. Without the benefit of any documents, he listed all of his siblings in the order of their birth, recalling most of their dates. I have added some dates of deaths that occurred after his memoir was written.

Juozas (Joseph), born 1902, died February 12, 1973; buried in Veiveriai cemetery.

Vladas, born October 5, 1903, died November 26,1984; buried in Veiveriai cemetery.

Adomas (Adam), born 1904, died 1939; buried in Rumbonys cemetery.

Antanas (Anthony), born 1906, died 1943 in Siberia.

Petras (Peter), born June 4, 1908, died April 13, 1993; buried in Kaunas.

Vaclovas, born and died about 1910 in infancy.

Kazimieras (Kazys), born February 27, 1912, died February 9, 2007; buried in Daytona Beach, Florida.

Teofilė, born 1914, died 1927; buried in Rumbonys cemetery.

Monika, born October 2, 1916, died November 27, 1979; buried in Veiveriai cemetery.

Onutė (Ann), born and died about 1918 in infancy.

Domicelė (called Damutė), born May 13, 1920, died January 10, 2011; buried in Šlienava cemetery (Kaunas district).

It's hard for us today to imagine how mother Magdalena remained cheerful and energetic while almost constantly pregnant for twenty years. Although the loss of two infants must have been painful, she suffered even more when three of her children died as young adults: daughter Teofilė at age 13, son Adomas at age 35, and son Antanas, age 37, who was exiled to Siberia and perished there with his wife and five children. In addition, she lost her son Kazys, whom she never saw again after he left Lithuania in 1944 at age 32. How did Magdalena raise this brood of children to be good human beings while living crowded together in a small cottage? As a farm wife she did the cooking and baking, but also plenty of farm work: she took care of animals, tended the vegetable and flower gardens, helped out on the fields at harvest time, preserved fruits and vegetables, spun and wove linen that became garments and bed sheets, washed the laundry by hand with water from a well. She taught her daughters how to knit warm clothes for the winter, to embroider their blouses in bright colors, to weave the beautiful traditional sashes and the linen for their dowry chests. Then there were the holidays and weddings that required special meals and decorations. In the long winter evenings, sitting by the wood-burning stove, Magdalena entertained her children with folk tales and ghost stories. She was not unique. Most Lithuanian farm women in the early part of the 20th century lived similar lives of hardship. How did they stay in good spirits under these conditions — singing, laughing, telling their children stories? We, their descendants, must wonder in amazement at the strength of these women.

Kazys wrote at length about each of the five brothers and the two sisters with whom he grew up, proceeding from oldest to youngest.

Juozas *(Joseph) had from his youth an inclination to technology and inventions. He did his work with elegance and precision. It's too bad he never had the opportunity for some theoretical training — he might have achieved real distinction in the field of technology. He did his military service in the Lithuanian army as a radio and telegraphy specialist in the Communications Division and then joined the Air Force as a non-commissioned officer. He later continued to work there as a civilian. In the Air Force he was highly regarded as a radio station mechanic. From 1927 he always lived in Kaunas, where in 1933 he married Marytė (Mary)* Juozas Baranauskas. *Kudirkaitė. They had two daughters: Irena (born 1934) and Laima (born 1936). After the Soviet occupation, Juozas made his living repairing private radios. This brother of mine was a very good person but not very strong-willed. He helped me a lot when I was studying.*

Klaus and I met Uncle Juozas when we visited Vilnius in 1969. He was a quiet, modest man. He had died by the time I returned to Lithuania in the summer of 1973. However, I met his two daughters, Irena and Laima, again. At that time, the relatives ostracized the younger sister, Laima, because she had married a Russian, a hated enemy. She and her husband came to see me separately from the others. Her husband was a gentle, soft-spoken eye doctor

who had been stationed in Vilnius with the Soviet Army. I learned later that they had moved to Leningrad because Laima's family refused to talk to her husband and, as one of the "occupiers," he felt resented in Lithuania. Although Laima and her husband Valerij and daughter Greta later returned to live in Kaunas, I never met

Brothers Vladas and Juozas, later in life.

Laima again. She died in 2011. Juozas' other daughter, Irena, received a Ph.D. in herbal medicine and taught at Kaunas University. She enjoyed taking her students into the forests of Lithuania to collect medicinal plants and she published professional articles as well as popular booklets on the use of these plants. Since our father always felt a debt of gratitude to his brother Juozas for supporting him during his studies, he and our mother invited Irena to visit the United States for a month in September 1988. Along with her came a cousin from our mother's side, Edvardas Bolisas. They stayed with our parents in Florida, visited Dana in Boston, Algis in New Hampshire, and also spent a week with Klaus and me in Cincinnati, Ohio. I will have more to say about that visit in a later chapter. Irena died in 1996, age 62.

Vladas *was talented and liked to study. A tall, good-looking man, he was a gifted speaker and enjoyed being among people. In 1929 he married Marytė Gurevičiūtė from the town of Marijampolė. Both were schoolteachers by profession. They had three children: Vytautas, Gražina, and Vida.*

By the time Klaus and I met Uncle Vladas in 1969, he had left his wife and children to live with a woman who was a school principal and Communist Party member. It's not surprising that an ambitious person joined the Communist Party in those days in order to advance in his/her career. However, this woman was the only seemingly convinced Communist whom I met among our relatives. She explained to us how much good the Communist system had done for Lithuania. I felt that she was a source of embarrassment for Uncle Vladas and everyone around her. Of Vladas' three children, the friendliest to us in America has been Gražina. She always wanted to meet anyone from the American branch who visited Lithuania and she has maintained a regular correspondence with us. Gražina and her pleasant husband

Vladas Baranauskas.

Antanas Lingis worked as horticulturalists for the city of Vilnius, responsible for the beautification of the parks and city streets. Both of them are intensely patriotic, politically engaged people, who hated the Russian occupation and the Communist system. Once, when I was walking down the street with her in Vilnius, while it was still Soviet, a person approached and asked her something in Russian. She just shrugged her shoulders and walked away. She and her husband Antanas were both very involved emotionally in the reestablishment of independence in 1990 and Gražina's letters to me were full of political commentary. All her life she suffered from poor health but she has a remarkable spirit, is well read, and has broad interests in music and culture. Their only child, son Giedrius Lingis, is an economist who works for the government. The family is close and loving.

I met Gražina's sister Vida, her husband Bronius, their daughter Vaida and son Audrius in Kaunas. However, the contact remained minimal. Gražina and Vida's brother Vytautas had a high-placed position as an engineer in a field that did not allow him to meet with people from the West. He sent us greetings by word of mouth when we visited. He died before the Soviet system collapsed.

On my second visit to Lithuania in 1973, I learned about a break that had developed between Vladas and his youngest sibling, Damutė. While I don't know the details, it involved the joint purchase of a small house. Vladas, by then a widower, expected to live in one part of the house with his sister's large family. This did not work out and Vladas felt bitter. He and his three children broke off all communication with Damutė and her family.

Adomas Baranauskas at age 26 in 1930.

Adomas (Adam), like Juozas, had an inclination for things technical and mechanical, completing his projects in a precise and attractive way. Although, he read widely, he unfortunately didn't have the opportunity for an education to develop his technical talents. He had a pleasant personality — the only brother with whom I could talk sincerely and openly about issues that concerned us. A great misfortune struck him when he was about 17. He developed an infection in one of his knees and since there was no medical help, the infection spread into the bone of the knee. Finally, an operation removed part of the bone, so that he could no longer bend the knee. Perhaps the operation came too late or was not done properly because he never recovered fully and the wound did not heal completely. After the operation, he spent an entire year in bed, unable to walk. When he recovered somewhat, he went back to doing hard physical labor on the farm, but various illnesses continued to torment him. Adomas died in the summer of 1939, just 35 years of age. He suffered greatly for eighteen years, in the prime of his life, yet he never complained. He had to maintain a strict diet, a difficult thing to do living on a farm. Nor was he able to drink alcohol or smoke. I still marvel at how he maintained his good humor under all these trials. I saw Adomas for the last time a few days before his death in the Alytus hospital. I lived in Kaunas at that time. Having received the final sacraments, he died peacefully, fully conscious to the end and comforting his weeping parents. We buried him in the cemetery at Rumbonys, next to his grandfather.

Antanas (Anthony) became an elementary school teacher. He was slow in temperament, modest and somewhat naïve. Although his abilities were just average, he made up for that with hard, conscientious work. He differed from the other brothers in his lack of critical judgment. Having just begun to teach, he married the first woman who came along, Stasė (Stanislava) Goštautaitė, and fell completely under her influence [...]. They had five children, all smart and capable, especially the oldest son Algirdas. During the mass deportations of June 14–15, 1941, the Bolsheviks arrested Antanas' family then living in the village of Bambininkai near Alytus. He himself was away from home at that time, visiting our parents, and could have survived. But upon learning that his family had been arrested, Antanas went home and gave himself up. He thought that in exile he would stay with his family and be able to take care of his wife and children. However, in retrospect we know that his heroic deed was meaningless because in Siberia the men were separated from the women and children. There was a rumor that Antanas had managed to escape from the train station in Vilnius but this proved to be false.

Our uncle and his family were transported in freight cars to Siberia, eventually to the Arctic Circle, for slave labor in a fishing camp. This primitive camp was on Trofimovsk Island located in the Lena River Delta. By chance, I translated into English an interview with a survivor who as a young girl was exiled to an island in the Lena River Delta. It may even have been the same Trofimovsk Island, although she does not give the name. Her interview is among several included in the film "Red Terror on the Amber Coast" that I mention again later. Her description of life there gives a clear idea of what our uncle and his family experienced before they perished. When the exiles disembarked, they found an island empty, desolate, with minimal vegetation. Under the

Kazys financed this memorial to his brother's family, which stands next to his mother's grave in Veiveriai. The inscription reads:

In memory of the Siberian deportees teacher Antanas Baranauskas, his wife Stasė and their five small children, who were deported in June 1941. They died of starvation in winter 1942, on the terrible island of Trofimovsk.

surface soil, the ground was permanently frozen. Their first task was to pull logs from the water to shore, to hew those logs and to build houses for the guards. The exiles were not allowed to use any of the logs for their own housing. Instead, they gathered branches, constructed frames and covered them with pieces of sod. These were their only shelters during the severe Arctic winter. Not only the adults but also the young children were forced to work under extremely difficult conditions. In the brutally cold Arctic climate, they lacked not only adequate shelter but also food and proper clothing. Since there was no medical help and people were weakened by starvation, illnesses spread quickly. The records of 488 Lithuanians who perished on Trofimovsk Island include the names of our relatives. Uncle Antanas and his wife Stasė died in 1942. Their children, son Algirdas (age 10), daughter Danguolė (age 8), twin daughters Gražina and Birutė (age 4), and infant son Rimantas (age 1) died in the winter of 1943.

By sending innocent people to their deaths in Siberia, Stalin established a reign of terror that was supposed to prevent resistance to Soviet rule in the Baltic States. Many of the people arrested and deported were considered "bourgeois" enemies of the Communist state because they had been in positions of leadership before the war, or were educated, or owned more property than the average. Perhaps they had made an anti-Soviet remark, had resisted the collectivization of their farm, or were denounced to the authorities by a jealous neighbor. For reasons such as these, about 50,000 Lithuanians out of a population of 3 million were deported by Stalin's regime during and after World War II. It is estimated that half of them perished. Our father Kazys, too, was on the list of people to be deported in 1941, as I will describe in a later chapter.

A historical novel told from the point of view of a young girl vividly describes the deportations and is helpful for understanding what happened to these people: "Between Shades of Gray" by Rūta Šepetys (2011). A documentary film, "Red Terror on the Amber Coast," released in 2008 and shown widely on PBS stations, describes the Soviet occupation of Lithuania and especially the deportations through eyewitness reports and interviews.

Petras *(Peter) differed from the rest of us brothers in several ways: he was quick-tempered, impulsive, with no interest or ability for study. However, he didn't drink or smoke and worked hard at achieving his goals. Against our parents' wishes he married Nastė Batiuškaitė from the village of Cibiliekai in the district of Odrija. She was the daughter of a farmer who owned much land but also was deeply in debt. She was similarly hot-tempered, so this marriage brought discord into our family. Because Petras now demanded his share of the inheritance, my father sold our homestead in Žaunieriškiai in 1938, bought a smaller and poorer farm in the village of Panemuninikai, paid off some debts, and gave the remaining money to Petras as his share. Although before his marriage Petras had been somewhat undependable, he turned out to be a loyal husband and good father. With his share of the inheritance, he developed some profitable skills. He learned how to make cement tiles for roofs, bought the necessary equipment and made a good living with this work in summer. In addition, he learned how to work with fur and leather, work that occupied the winter months. But after Adomas died in 1939, since no other brother was available to help, our father invited Petras to take over the management of the farm. Petras had two daughters and a son. [Rūta, Dalia, and Gediminas]*

Petras with his second wife Stefanija.

After my father died, mother continued to live on the farm with Petras and his family. Knowing the difficult nature of Petras' wife, I imagine that my mother's situation was not a happy one. Having raised a large number of children and suffering from poor health, she did not receive the care and respect she deserved. I also blame myself for that. When the Soviets occupied Lithuania a second time (1944), they again deported many Lithuanians to Siberia, among them Petras. He was arrested in May of 1948 and brought to a forest-cutting camp near the Abakan River, about 300 km north of the town of Abakan. When he returned from exile in 1958, he found his wife living with another man. He divorced her, remarried, and settled in Palemonas near Kaunas.

On an early visit to Lithuania, either in 1969 or 1973, I met Uncle Petras and his second wife Stefanija. He struck me as a cheerful, good-humored person with a positive attitude in spite of the hardships he had endured. When I asked him about his ten years of exile in Siberia, he shrugged his shoulders and said, "It wasn't so bad… I survived." In the spring of 2013, when Klaus and I attended a Baranauskas family reunion, we learned that Petras' son Gediminas was still living on the same farm in Panemunininkai. I also heard a different explanation as to why Kazys' father Antanas lost the family homestead in Žaunieriškiai and was forced to move to a poorer farm in Panemunininkai. According to my relatives' account, Antanas had agreed to help an individual he trusted obtain a bank loan. The bank demanded Antanas' farm as collateral on the debt. The borrower defaulted and Antanas was left holding the bag. The bank took possession of the farm in Žaunieriškiai so Antanas was forced to move to the smaller, poorer one in Panemunininkai. My cousins did not know who defaulted on the loan but it must have been someone whom Antanas felt obliged to help. A guess on my part: perhaps it was Petras' father-in-law Batiuškis, who, according to Kazys, had a lot of land and a lot of debts.

The two sisters, Damute and Monika.

Monika and *Damutė*, both very dear sisters, had good voices and liked to sing. Monika was the quieter of the two — skilled in handicrafts and an excellent cook. Damutė as the youngest was a bit spoiled by everyone...she grew up carefree and cheerful. She started to study at the agricultural academy in Alytus but gave it up when she met a student of forestry, Antanas Rėklaitis. When he finished his schooling in 1940, they married and settled in Kazlų Rūda, a town surrounded by vast forests. They had five sons [Arvydas, Eligijus, Juozas, Valdas, Edmundas]. Monika married Juozas Atmanavičius in the same year, 1940. The two had been in love for some time. He was a farmer in the village of Panemunininkai, a well-read, pleasant, and courteous person. They had two sons and one daughter [Gintautas, Rimas, Danguolė].

On our visits to Lithuania, Klaus and I met both of father's sisters and developed close contacts with their families.

Kazys' Memories of World War I

When our father was born on February 27, 1912, Lithuania was still a part of the Russian empire ruled by the Czar. Russia had ruled Lithuania since 1795 when the great powers, Prussia, Austria, and Russia, partitioned the Commonwealth of Poland-Lithuania among themselves. When World War I broke out in 1914, the German army occupied Poland and Lithuania on its way into Russia. Kazys' earliest memories went back to the summer of 1915 when his family fled from the approaching German army.

As the German army approached Lithuania, the retreating Russians urged the population to move east, away from the line of battle. Especially people living along the Nemunas River felt threatened because it was thought that the Russian army would use the river to make a stand. Kazys' parents loaded their most necessary possessions on a wagon, hitched up a pair of horses, took their children and left home. Only great-grandfather Jurgis remained behind, refusing to leave the family homestead under any circumstances. Kazys, three years old at the time, remembered this flight from home:

I remember clearly how they lifted me on top of the loaded wagon, how we crossed the Nemunas River in rowboats. We drove to the village of Lelioniai, district of Butrimoniai, to stay with my mother's uncle Žilinskas. I remember how we all climbed into a pit in a field, a pit that had been dug to store potatoes for the winter. From the distance we heard the rumble of cannon fire. When the battlefront passed, we returned home. As it turned out, no major battles took place in our area thus the farms were not destroyed. But many people who were caught up in the stream of refugees fleeing east ended up deep inside Russia and returned home only after the war ended. These people experienced all the horrors of the Bolshevik Revolution and came back in tatters. They found their homes and farms dilapidated and neglected.

In some cases, the fleeing Russians set fire to the Lithuanian villages so that the Germans could not use the dwellings for shelter. As soon as the war started, Lithuanian young men were pulled into the Russian army. Those too young to fight were forced to dig trenches. Nonetheless, most of the rural population in Lithuania sympathized with the Russian side, not the German. In the 120 years of Russian rule, people had become accustomed to the Czarist Empire. After serfdom was abolished, the standard of living had improved. In the aftermath of the 1905 revolution, Lithuania received some cultural and political rights. Since many of the "excess" youth emigrated to America, they either returned with savings or sent money home to their relatives. For these reasons, people accepted Russian rule and feared the unknown Germans.

In our father's memory, the German occupation during World War I was very difficult for the rural population. The occupying Germans treated Lithuania as enemy territory, publishing rules and regulations designed to extract fees and supplies from the farmers. They confiscated horses and other animals. If a farmer wanted to slaughter a pig, he had to obtain a permit, then give up most of the meat to the administration. People tried to avoid these regulations by hiding their animals and slaughtering them in secret. The occupying troops cut down the forests and shipped the trees off to Germany. Since there was no oil, people split pine branches into narrow strips and used them to provide some light at night.

The Germans took away our better horses, leaving only young ones not able to do much fieldwork. They left us only one old cow. As a result, our harvest was poor but the family large: grandparents, parents, and eight children — 12 mouths to feed. The older children were adolescents while the younger ones still babies. We didn't get enough milk from that old cow and hardly ever saw meat. Our diet was mostly bread, potatoes, and vegetables. And we children had appetites like wolves. […] But my mother knew how to prepare healthy meals even out of simple products. She wove the linen cloth herself and sewed our clothes by hand. She worked day and night to keep us children fed and clothed.

During World War I, Lithuania's farmers became impoverished. It took them at least a decade to recover some semblance of normal life.

Chapter 3: Kazys Struggles for an Education

Although Kazys was a bright, eager student, who did well in school, he had to interrupt his education early, after completing only four and a half grades. The primary difficulty was that his parents lacked the financial resources to educate so many children. It seemed that he had no alternative but to remain on the farm and work in the fields alongside his father. However, Kazys was not satisfied with such a future. He applied remarkable willpower to study on his own and to pass the secondary school exams that would allow him to enter a technical college with a scholarship. He described this struggle for an education in considerable detail in his memoir. He was truly a self-made man and was proud of this achievement all of his life. The details that he remembered into old age are remarkable, in particular the names of his teachers. He acknowledged how important they were in his development.

Under Russian rule and German occupation there were few schools in the rural areas, usually just one school in an entire district. The closest school for us was located in the village of Dubėnai, about 4 km to the northwest from Žaunieriškiai. Since children walked to school on foot, they could only start school when they were somewhat older, between 10 and 12 years old. In my father's generation, almost all the sons finished elementary school, but only a few farmers sent their daughters to school. The girls were taught at home to read from a prayer book and that was the extent of their education. My mother, too, knew only how to read but not to write. All children born after 1900, boys as well as girls, attended elementary school.

More schools were built as soon as Lithuania regained independence (1918). The first school in our village was established in 1919. My Uncle Jonas (John) provided his parlor as space for the classroom (for which he was compensated by the district) and the farmers got together to build the school benches. A woman had just returned from Russia where she had taught in an orphanage during the war. She had completed several years of secondary school and had taken some additional courses. This Emilija Paulauskaitė became our first teacher. In the fall of 1919 I started first grade, however I had already learned to read at home. Two years later the school was relocated to the village of Miklusėnai, 4 km to the southwest from Žaunieriškiai. Every day I walked to that school with brother Petras. During the winter, to shorten the way, we walked through the fields. Since I was then just nine years old, this was quite a trip for me. In those days no one wore shoes during the week, and we children didn't have any real shoes at all. We walked around with wooden clogs that quickly filled up with snow. When I'd find a large rock or clod of earth, I'd knock the snow out and continue walking. All day we sat in school with wet feet — I'm amazed we didn't get sick. However, these were just the minor problems. Our biggest fear was that we might meet up with a crazy man who roamed the area and liked to scare children. Then there were the loose dogs, some of them infected with rabies. The teacher in the Miklusėnai school was Jurgis Krygeris who had graduated from the teachers' college in Veiveriai. But he wasn't much interested in teaching since he had a farm in the village of Bakšiai that took up most of his time. I did not learn much that year.

For the following academic year, 1922/23, school was reopened in Žaunieriškiai and that is where I completed the final year of elementary school, the third grade. Our teacher was Vaclovas Bartlingas, a nephew of Adomas Balynas. He had completed five years of secondary school and had studied at a seminary for the priesthood but left before finishing it. He was an idealistic person who loved his pupils and seldom punished us. With his kind manners he stimulated our interest and we children loved and respected him. He gave me a solid foundation in the basic subjects so that in the following fall (1923) I easily passed the entrance exams to the secondary school in Alytus.

This secondary school had been founded in 1918 or 1919 in former army barracks. Until 1923 its first principal was Kazys Klimavičius. Initially, there were only four classes but each year an additional class was added, so that by 1926 it was a full secondary school with eight classes. My brother Vladas completed the fourth class in the spring of 1923 and received an offer to teach elementary school in the town of Merkinė. When I entered this school, my brother Antanas was in the third class. In fall and spring we walked together to school on foot, a distance of about six or seven kilometers. Only in winter, when there was too much snow, my parents arranged lodging for us in town. That first year we lived in the Marcinkevičius home on Seirijai Street. In addition to my brother and me, five other students and three adults shared the space, ten people in two rooms plus kitchen. My parents brought food products from home, while the woman of the house cooked them. We never had quite enough to eat. [...] Nonetheless, I did well in my studies.

Because of the difficult living conditions, tuberculosis spread easily among the students and every year a number of young people died. When I was in the second class, I too began to cough in a suspicious way so that my parents became concerned about my health. They were also finding it difficult to pay the expenses of two students at the same time. In the middle of the second year I had to leave the secondary school. Thus ended the first stage of my education.

Back on the farm, Kazys, along with the other children, was sent out in summer to herd animals, a chore he did not like. It was hard to get up very early in the morning to bring the animals out to pasture. And it was boring to watch the animals and make sure they did not wander off into the grain fields. As soon as the children started some interesting game, the animals started to cause problems. But after the noonday meal the herding was done and they were free to spend the afternoons as they wished. They immediately ran off to the banks of the Nemunas River to play. According to our father, the landscape was beautiful: the banks of the river were covered with various bushes; pine trees grew on the slopes. The Nemunas had dug a deep channel so the slopes were steep and many smaller creeks created deep gullies. Kazys remembered that he spent the best hours of his boyhood here, playing on the banks of the river. As he got older, he was given other, more demanding work to do on the farm.

Although Kazys felt stuck on the farm, he developed various pastimes to keep his mind stimulated. His favorite activity was reading:

Kazys loved the theater all his life and was a talened actor. Here he played the main role, the bearded old man sitting in the front row. Photo taken in 1932.

From early on, I felt a great attraction to books. I read whatever I could get my hands on. Books stimulated my desire for a better, more enlightened existence. Music also attracted me and at one point I decided to learn to play the violin. Having saved a few litai [Lithuanian currency], I bought a homemade violin and together with a friend went to Adomas Balynas for lessons. I started to learn with great enthusiasm, soon knew the notes and could play simple tunes. But I wasn't able to make much progress. I learned from this experience that in the arts effort is not enough; one also needs inborn talent. After a while, I put my violin aside.

His best friend in the village was a boy of the same age, Jurgis (George) Gavelis, who had finished three years in secondary school but like Kazys was unable to study further. The two boys met often to talk and dream. Life on the farm was dull, without the challenges they craved. Yet they had so much potential within them and so much energy. Where should they direct it?

Jurgis Gavelis was Kazys' best friend. Photo taken in 1933,

Driven by our restlessness, we distracted ourselves with nightly dances, looking for love and conquest. We read Knut Hamsun's "Vagabonds"[1] and envied the characters in that novel. We grabbed every opportunity to escape our monotonous surroundings. We even tried to volunteer for the army but they would not take us. One windy fall Sunday in 1932 I got on my bike and prepared to ride to Alytus. I had to find some way to liven up my day. But the wind was blowing so hard against me that it was almost impossible to ride forward. Just then I noticed that my friend Jurgis was heading toward our house. So I turned around and went back. We sat down in the orchard, sheltered from the wind; my brother Adomas joined us, and we started to talk. The idea came up in our conversation that Jurgis and I should take up our studies again — prepare at home, then take the exams to complete at least four classes of secondary school. After that we would see what else we could do.

Jurgis promised to get hold of the necessary textbooks from students at the secondary school — from the girl students, of course, since he was very good-

---

[1] Knut Hamsun (1859–1952), a Norwegian author, won the Nobel Prize for literature in 1920. His novel "Vagabonds" (1909) develops the theme of a perpetual wanderer, a stranger who enters into the life of a small rural community. Hamsun portrayed a deep, romantic connection between his characters and nature.

looking and therefore popular with them. Later, I went to get advice from Adomas Balynas. He told me, "your plan is a good one — you just need to act on it." He probably thought that I would not have the determination to do it. After some initial enthusiasm the whole thing would be forgotten. To tell the truth, I also wondered some times whether I could achieve this plan under the circumstances. And these circumstances were really difficult. I had time to study only after the farm work was done, in the evenings and on Sundays. The only source of light at night was a kerosene lamp and the kerosene was expensive. After reading for hours with such a lamp my eyes became tired. Besides, the textbooks I had borrowed were mostly old and didn't match exactly the subject matter covered in the secondary school at this time. Even worse, I didn't have any textbooks at all for some of the courses. Jurgis and I agreed not to talk to anyone about our plans, so that we would not look foolish in case we failed.

At that time I was fully immersed in the social life of the young people in the area, going to all the amusements and festivities. Once I started to study, I had to separate myself from my friends and stop going to the parties. That was not easy. I have a character trait that has helped me reach my goals in life: if I decide to do something that is close to my heart, I then put my whole soul into it. All my thoughts focus on that goal, and before I know it, I have done it. So in this case too, I threw myself completely into this project. And a strong sense of duty led me to complete a job, once I had started it.

I started to smoke now and then when I was about 14 years old, at first in secret because my father forbade it, although he was a smoker himself. I started out of boredom, while herding animals with my friends and having nothing to do. By the time I was twenty, I was a serious smoker and I smoked in public. I grew the tobacco myself. Although I knew it was a bad habit, I could not decide to give it up. That fall, in 1932, when Jurgis and I decided to study, we agreed to quit smoking and use the money that we spent on cigarettes and tobacco for buying books and notebooks. We were waiting for a special occasion to start our no-smoking resolution. That came when we welcomed in the New Year 1933, at the home of Vincas Baranauskas in the village of Bakšiai. We went to the party together and smoked several cigarettes one after the other "for the last time" before making the resolution to quit. I kept my resolution for three years, while Jurgis managed just three weeks. The same thing happened with our studying: he never really started so I was left alone with the plan.

I didn't find it hard to master the four-year curriculum for religion, Lithuanian language, history, and geography. But to figure out mathematics, physics, and German without a teacher was much harder. If I could not solve a problem when tired in the evening, I would try it again early in the morning and usually succeeded. The exams were scheduled for June 1933. Thus I had *about six months to learn the entire curriculum of four years of secondary school. I often thought how easy it should be for the students who sit in class, who have all the textbooks, who get help from their teachers, who aren't interrupted by other work, and who have four years to learn all this. They must be lazy deadbeats if they complain that this is too hard. When I went into the fields to plow or harrow, I carried a book along. When I stopped the horses to give them a rest, I'd pull the book out and read. Then while working, I'd repeat in my head what I had read. That's the way I memorized German grammar. If I really couldn't figure out something myself, I would go to Mr. Balynas for help, or to a more advanced student who lived nearby.*

I had to take the exams[2] at the secondary school in Alytus whose principal at that time was Mr. Vaitkevičius and the school superintendent Kazys Klimavičius, a good friend of Adomas Balynas. It cost me 15 litai to take the exams, money that my father gave me with great reluctance. He must have thought that I would probably not pass the exams, and even if I did, what good would that do? Just a waste of money. I did pass the exams, but with an unexpected twist. [...] During the exams, Mr. Klimavičius, the superintendent, came by to see how it was going. Just at that moment, I was taking the physics exam. The topic was light rays and their application to photography. I only knew as much about this topic as I had learned from the textbook. Cameras were rare in those days and I had never had one in my hands. I don't remember the teacher's name only that she was unpleasant. She kept asking me more and more questions, beyond what was in the textbook and beyond what I knew. Then Mr. Klimavičius spoke up, "Madam, the questions you are asking are not from the curriculum of the fourth class but from the sixth." The teacher then concluded, "All right. You passed the exam but you're not much of a photographer."

As we will see later, a similar thing happened to me while I was taking the entrance exams for the technical college. As I conclude my life's journey, I see how in critical situations God helped me through good people.

Having earned the four-year secondary school certificate, Kazys wondered what to do next. Having come this far, he did not want to fall back to life on the farm. He knew he could not count on any help from home. A worldwide economic crisis had undermined Lithuania's farmers, including his father, who could no longer make ends meet. There were only a few colleges that accepted students with a four-year certificate. Among them was a horticultural college near Kaunas, the top choice for Kazys. So he hopped on his bike and peddled to Kaunas to talk to his older brother Juozas who was already employed as a

---

[2] Important exams such as these were in those days almost always oral and public, with several teachers present in the room.

radio technician in the Ministry of Aviation. Since Juozas was greatly attracted to technology, he urged Kazys to apply to the Technical College in Kaunas and offered to let him live with him and his family. Even though Kazys did not feel inclined in that direction and would have preferred to study horticulture, he had no choice but to accept his brother's offer.

The Technical College in Kaunas, supported by the Ministry of Communications, had high academic standards with a course of study that took five years. The College accepted students who, like our father, had only a four-year certificate, but required them to pass an entrance exam in mathematics and the Lithuanian language. There were many candidates for just a few places so the exams were demanding. Our father had the misfortune of being examined by an instructor of mathematics named Mr. Šernas, whose name means "Boar" and whom the students universally feared. This Šernas flunked Kazys in geometry, because, as our father explained, "I had not used the right textbook in my preparation." When Kazys returned to try the geometry exam a second time there were only two places left and about 50 candidates. Šernas did not agree to let Kazys try again because he had already failed once. But then, an unexpected thing happened:

I went back to the office to pick up my documents and was prepared to return home a failure. Then I remembered that I had left my hat on the desk in the exam room so I returned to pick it up. I sat down at the desk to watch the exams in progress because I was reluctant to go home. Who would believe me that there were not enough places left... everyone would assume I failed the exam again. In the meantime, Šernas was running through the candidates quickly. Whoever made even a minor mistake was dismissed. When he finished with the list of candidates, he asked, "Is there anyone here who wants to try a second time?" I stood up. Šernas, who seemed not to like me, was unhappy but could not back away from his offer. Having prepared myself thoroughly this time, I gave clear and precise answers to all the questions. This attracted the attention of the college director, Mr. Gravrokas, who was observing the exams. Even though I was answering correctly, Šernas continued to be dissatisfied and continued to ply me with questions. Finally the director said to Šernas, "That's enough. He has passed the exam very well." This is how I was chosen for one of the two open positions.

Šernas, however, resented Kazys from then on. Since our father always did well in his math courses, Šernas couldn't do anything against him. But finally, he had his revenge. Without any cause or provocation, he lowered our father's grade for conduct. This caused Kazys to lose his tuition scholarship for a semester. A few months into his studies, Kazys was about to drop out of college because he did not have the 50 litai for that semester's tuition. He did not want to ask Juozas for the money because his brother was already providing him with room and board. At the very last minute his brother Vladas sent him the money.

Kazys felt that an "invisible hand" had guided him in his studies and into his profession of electrical engineering. Initially he felt handicapped by the lack of a systematic secondary school preparation, but with determined effort he rose to the ranks of the top students at the college. Brother Juozas continued to provide him with room and board, while during the summer he was able to earn some money through internships. By saving every penny he managed to pay for necessary school expenses and for his clothing. Starting with the third year, he received a tuition waiver and a partial scholarship of 40 litai a month — a great help. This episode in his life confirmed for him the proverb that, "Every beginning is difficult" and one should not lose hope even in the most difficult circumstances.

Kazys in uniform.

The summer of 1936 brought a serious setback — Kazys received a draft notice from the military. He had completed the third year of electrical engineering and was working that summer as an intern in the construction of an automated telephone station in Kaunas. Normally, students were given military deferments. Probably because Kazys was older and approaching the end of the draftable age, the military authorities drafted him before he finished his studies. The Alytus Draft Board declared him fit for service and at his request assigned him to serve in the signal corp. Kazys felt that this area of service would be closest to his studies. On November 4, 1936 he reported for duty at the signal corps barracks located in a Kaunas suburb. The commander of the signal corps was Lieutenant Vitkauskas, an exact and pedantic person who demanded strict discipline, especially from the new recruits. Any infraction of the rules or lack of cleanliness led to hours of penalty work. Kazys decided to avoid these penalties at all cost, so he even stopped smoking to have more time to get all his required work done properly. He was proud of the fact that in his entire service time he managed to avoid all reprimands and penalties.

After finishing basic training he was assigned to the radiotelegraphy group for six months of instruction. This is the period of military service that he enjoyed most. He made a close friend, a former teacher named Jonas Dvariškis, with whom he shared all joys and sorrows. He finished this training in second place and received an award, an attractive pocket watch. After that he was assigned to the signal corps workshops where the work was boring.

When he started his service in the signal corps workshops in the fall of 1937, Kazys realized that he might be able to resume his studies at the technical college. He was free in the evenings and the fourth-year courses at the college were scheduled in the evenings. But it took several months to get permission from the military authorities. By the time he came to Director Gravrokas with the request to resume classes, the academic year was in full swing. The director doubted that it would work out. Not only had the classes started, but Kazys had been gone for a year and thus forgotten a lot. Besides, since he was busy all day with his military service, he would have no time to prepare for his classes. But the

Kazys during military serivice (on the right).

director finally agreed to let him try. The situation was really very difficult, as Kazys describes it:

When I finished my service work for the day, I had only twenty minutes to get to the classes. I had to quickly change into civilian clothes and reach the college, which was about two miles away. If I missed the bus, I had to run all the way. At first, I really did not understand what the instructor was saying... the course had started some time ago. By the time I returned to the barracks it was about 11 at night. I did my course preparations during the class breaks and on Sundays. At first I asked my classmates when I didn't understand something, but after several months of intense work, they came to me for help. I finished the fourth year as one of the top students. When the director saw the year-end results, he kept repeating, "I didn't expect this."

I finished my military service in spring 1938 with the rank of sergeant and joined the reserves. That summer I was in desperate need of money, so I worked during the day doing electrical installations for private customers and at night at a Kaunas radio station. At the start of my last academic year in fall 1938, the college moved to new and better quarters on Tvirtovė Boulevard in Kaunas. I now received a full scholarship of 80 litai per month. This amount was enough to cover my living expenses so I rented an attractive room close to the school. It would have been too far for me to walk from Juozas' home. This last year of college was the happiest for me, and in spring 1939 I graduated with honors as valedictorian.

After finishing his studies, Kazys and a friend worked privately for a while as electrical installers. Then, still in 1939, he joined a semi-governmental agency "Elektra" whose task was to build up the electrical network in Lithuania. "Elektra" sent him and a student to Latvia for a month to get acquainted with the Keguma power plant and with the construction of power lines. In his work with "Elektra" he was responsible for construction projects that brought electricity from the Latvian power plant to villages in northern Lithuania. This work made our father happy since he knew he was improving the lives of farmers in villages like his own.

Chapter 4:
Lithuania – the Historical Context

Independent Lithuania, 1918–1940

Lithuania gained its independence from Russia in 1918 due to a combination of favorable circumstances. First, the Russian Czarist regime was weakened by World War I and then overthrown by the Bolsheviks. In that power vacuum Lithuanians quickly proclaimed their independence on February 16, 1918 and established their own government for the first time in more than 120 years. A Lithuanian volunteer army fought and expelled various bands of German and Russian troops that had remained behind after the war. Although this independence lasted only 22 years, it formed the context for our father's youth and growth to manhood; it formed his social values and political convictions. Kazys spent many pages of his memoir describing the historical context in which he lived, and although the facts can be found in history books, it's interesting to see how he viewed events and how these events shaped his life.

Kazys described the independence period positively as a time of economic and cultural revival. Along with rapid change and modernization came a sense of national identity and a surge in patriotism, especially among idealistic young people. At the start of independence, Lithuania was an agrarian country, with small towns, almost no industry, a poor infrastructure, and underdeveloped commerce. The two largest cities were Vilnius, the ancient capital, and Kaunas. However, in 1920 Poland occupied Vilnius and surrounding districts by force, claiming that this area was historically a part of Poland. Kaunas became Lithuania's "temporary capital" and its only significant city. The lack of industry meant a lack of jobs for young people who needed to leave the farms. Since the USA closed its doors to immigration after World War I, many young men left to find work in South America, especially in Brazil. Recruiters arrived to promise free travel and work on sugar or coffee plantations. Then in 1930 an economic crisis bankrupted many farmers as the prices for farm products dropped suddenly. Kazys gave some dramatic examples: 50 kg of grain fell from 25 litai to 5; the price for a fattened hog weighing about 90 kg fell from about 150 litai to 30. And even then, farmers had trouble selling their animals.

The Lithuanian government came to the aid of farmers to help them become more competitive on the world market. Whereas prior to 1930 Lithuanian agriculture was dominated by grain production, the farmers learned to diversify into animal husbandry, dairy, and other products. The government established cooperatives that provided farmers with investment capital, expertise, machinery, and fertilizer. The cooperatives bought up products, exported them, and established a modern food processing industry. An agricultural reform carried out at the beginning of independence broke up large estates that had belonged to the gentry. The lands were divided among volunteers who had fought for independence and among landless farm workers. Education improved with the establishment of many types of schools: elementary, secondary, vocational, and college. Newspapers developed mass circulations as farmers began to subscribe widely. The appearance of the towns and cities changed: they were cleaned up and beautified, many new buildings were constructed, the arts flourished. An improved infrastructure of roads and power lines covered the rural areas and the farm population began to recover and prosper.

Kazys described these rapid changes with pride: in 22 short years Lithuanians made revolutionary changes in the economy of their country. They built a modern country from the ground up. They did it themselves, without help from the outside, and by peaceful means, without the bloodshed and civil war that marked the communist revolution in Russia.

Kazys criticized one political development that, in his view, was a mistake. Lithuania's short experiment with democracy ended in December 1926 when a military coup installed one-party rule under the authoritarian president Antanas Smetona. The National Party ("Tautininkai") banned opposition parties and preserved its power with the support of the military, with press censorship, and by means of nepotism, and corruption. But Kazys felt that this flirtation with dictatorship was relatively benign compared to the Stalinist, Nazi, and fascist dictatorships that came to power at this time in other European countries.

Kazys' formative years in independent Lithuania developed in him a great love of country and pride in its accomplishments on the one hand, and on the other hand a fierce hatred of Communism and those who brought it to Lithuania. The rapid progress he saw in those years confirmed his natural optimism — the confidence that he can accomplish anything he sets his mind to do. He firmly believed that people could improve themselves and their community through initiative and honest hard work.

The Occupations of Lithuania

In World War II Lithuania was repeatedly invaded and occupied by its powerful neighbors from the East and the West. First came the Soviet army in June 1940. A year later, in June 1941, the Germans went to war with the Soviet Union and marched into Lithuania, driving out the Russians and occupying Lithuania for three years. Then, in the summer of 1944, the Soviet army returned, drove out the Germans and established Communist rule in our country that was to last for almost 50 years, until 1990. One can imagine the suffering of the Lithuanian population who lived through this chaotic time.

Before they went to war with each other, the two dictators, Hitler and Stalin, divided up Eastern Europe between themselves in a secret protocol of the Molotov-Ribbentrop Pact that they signed in August 1939. According to this protocol, Poland, Lithuania, Latvia, Estonia, Finland, and Romania were divided into German and Soviet spheres of influence. Hitler and Stalin gave each other permission to invade these countries — and they immediately proceeded to do that.

The First Soviet Occupation, 1940–41

When the Soviet army invaded in 1940, Kazys described the reaction in Lithuania as uncertain — people did not know what to expect. Communism promised fairness and equality to all, an end to privileged social classes. This appealed to some Lithuanians who had no knowledge or experience of Communism as it was actually practiced by the Soviets. To many it seemed like the better alternative to Nazi rule. But very soon Lithuanians felt the terrible consequences. Arrests began immediately — people who held responsible positions in government or industry were jailed. Private property and businesses were confiscated; all Lithuanian organizations were banned, even nonpolitical ones like a stamp collectors' association; unqualified party loyalists took over leadership positions. A bureaucratic apparatus with all kinds of new rules and regulations was established and used to intimidated people.

The ordinary Russian soldiers who arrived in Lithuania believed they were introducing a better system. Much to their surprise, they found a country that was more prosperous and advanced than their own. They could not believe their eyes when they saw the great amount and variety of goods in the stores. They started to call Lithuania "Little America" and began to empty the stores of everything they could get their hands on.

The Bolsheviks turned the firm for which Kazys worked, "Elektra," into a governmental Department of Energy. They ordered "Elektra" to take over all the power plants in the country that were owned by municipalities or private individuals, to list all of the assets and to determine their value. According to Kazys, to do this task properly would have required at least three months, but the "Elektra" staff were given three days, a ridiculous demand that produced nothing but chaos.

In spring 1941 Kazys moved from Kaunas to Šiauliai, a town in northern Lithuania close to the Latvian border, where he was appointed director of power plant construction for the district. He rented a small, unfurnished room, found some primitive furniture and set to work. Soon he was frustrated, however, by a Soviet system demanding endless paperwork — all materials had to be listed, detailed work schedules drawn up,

Inž. Baranauskas Kazys

Šiaulių Elektrinių Rajono Tinklų Skyriaus
Viršininkas

Tel. 1431

Business card naming Kazys Director for the Šiauliai region power net.

forms filled out for every small item.... he could hardly do any productive work.

Many Lithuanians, horrified and frightened by the Soviet chaos and intimidation, yearned to escape. For some, an opportunity presented itself to pass as ethnic Germans and emigrate to Germany. According to the Molotov-Ribbentrop Pact, people of German descent living in countries occupied by the Soviets were allowed to "repatriate." When German representatives arrived in Lithuania to facilitate the repatriation, people lined up who had a German last name, those who had a German spouse, even those who merely belonged to the Protestant Church. These people were permitted to take out with them only what they could carry. Even so, about 50,000 people, many with false documents, chose to "repatriate" at that time. Father's best friend from child-hood, Jurgis Gavelis, with whom he had made the pact to resume his studies, was able to leave for Germany because his wife was of German descent.

As Lithuanians yearned for an end to the Soviet occupation, rumors spread in spring 1941 that Hitler's Germany would soon go to war against the Soviet Union. About June 10, a BBC broadcast announced that Germany was massing its army at the Soviet border and that war was imminent. This raised people's hopes that the Soviets would be kicked out and Lithuania would regain its freedom. They had no inkling of the atrocities the Communists still had in store for them. In order to strengthen their hold on the lands they had occupied, the Stalinists had made plans to exile to Siberia the entire elite of each country. From Lithuania they intended to deport about 750,000, a quarter of the population. State Security General Ivan Aleksandrovich Serov was put in charge of planning the deportations from the Baltic States. These plans were prepared with great secrecy.

One evening, it must have been June 13 [1941], I stopped in a café where I saw a man I knew from the town of Radviliškis. He told me in whispers that he had seen many freight cars in the train station prepared to take people away, Sure enough, early the next morning I witnessed a terrible sight in the streets of Šiauliai. Trucks with armed Russian soldiers were driving through the streets. In each truck was a civilian Communist party member who carried a list of people to be deported. They stormed into houses, ordered people to dress quickly, to pack a small bundle and to take some food. They loaded entire families into the trucks: parents, children, old people. They even took sick people, pregnant women, newborn infants. In some cases they dragged people out of hospitals. There was fear and crying throughout the town, as though the Last Judgment Day had arrived. People didn't know why or where they were being taken. Those arrested were brought to the nearest train station and loaded into freight cars, the kind used to transport animals. The wagons were bare inside with just a hole in the floor for eliminating human waste. It took several days to fill all the train cars and in the meantime those people crowded inside were exposed to the summer heat. We can imagine how those people suffered without sufficient water. Armed solders did not let anyone approach the wagons but in some cases children were able to sneak up and hand bottles of water to people inside. Under these conditions, many people perished during the transport. I knew an engineer from Šiauliai, Mr. Rudis, who went crazy. In just a few days, the Soviets deported about 40,000 people from Lithuania. I didn't feel much danger for myself because I had just arrived in Šiauliai and not many people knew me yet. But to be prepared in case they came for me, I packed a small bag with some essential things.

Although the Soviets did not have time to reach their goal of deporting a quarter of the population, they killed or shipped to Siberia more than 40,000 people just before the Germans began their invasion into Lithuania. On June 20, Kazys traveled on business to the town of Panevėžys to hire an engineer, Petras Ruibys, whom he knew from the technical college. He was spending the night with friends but their sleep was disturbed before dawn by a noise that sounded like thunder. Yet how could it be thunder? — the sky was clear. Soon they realized they were hearing German planes bombing the nearby Soviet airport. Kazys and his friend Petras Ruibys immediately left for Šiauliai.

What happened next in Šiauliai is a dramatic story of survival. It is a story that everyone in our family heard a number of times, although our parents did not talk about the war often. As I remember the oral version, Kazys and a couple of administrators of "Elektra" in Šiauliai received a secret warning via friends that their names had appeared on a list of people to be arrested. They decided to go into hiding, knowing that the days of the Soviets in Lithuania were numbered. The German army was already close by. They chose as their hiding place a newly built power plant outside of Šiauliai. In his memoir, Kazys described the motivation differently. He didn't mention the intent to hide; rather he said they went to protect the power plant from being destroyed by the retreating Russians. His version is clearly the more heroic one. Whatever the motivation, their decision saved them from certain deportation and, most likely, death. Here is the story in Kazys' own words:

In the evening [of the day when he and engineer Petras Ruibys returned to Šiauliai] Snarskis, the director of the power plant, Teleiša, the administrator, the above mentioned Ruibys, and I set off on foot to the newly built power plant on Rekyva Lake, about 8 kilometers south of Šiauliai. Our goal was to somehow protect the power plant from the retreating Russians who might try to blow it up. Among us we had but one pistol and a few bullets. Arriving in Rekyva, we shut down the plant so there would be less damage in case of an explosion. After that, we waited to see what would happen.

Not long after, a troop of Russian soldiers surrounded the power plant and forced their way into the yard. We four men quickly hid in an underground tunnel through which water flowed into the lake. Soon we heard footsteps and conversation above us. One of us climbed up a ladder wanting to see through a hole in the manhole cover what the Russians were doing. Just then, one of the soldiers stuck his bayonet into that same hole in an attempt to lift the cover, almost striking our friend in the eye. Our friend started to fall from the ladder — we grabbed him in time to keep him from landing in the water and making a big splash. The soldier was unable to lift the heavy metal cover. It was not the one we had opened to get into the tunnel but a heavier one. We heard him say in Russian, "This is closed." We, in the meantime, crawled into a pipe that went out into the lake. Soon we heard someone wading along the lakeshore and heard him say in Russian, "There's a tunnel here." But he did not bother to enter it.

After some time, the plant workers opened the cover and told us the Russians were gone. When we climbed out, we saw that the plant supervisor was pale as he wiped the sweat from his face. He told us what had happened. When the Russians entered the plant, they confronted him with the question, "Where are your administrators?" He told them the administrators were not present at this time. Then the Russians ordered him to call together all the workers. When everyone had gathered, the Russians asked, "Is everyone here?" He said yes. Then the Russians said they would look for themselves. The supervisor began to sweat, imagining what would happen if they found us.

This incident amazes me — the plant workers risked their own lives to protect their bosses. They all knew where the four men were hiding but not one of them weakened under pressure to betray them. Because of this remarkable solidarity, Kazys and his co-workers survived the first Soviet occupation.

A few days later, the first German soldiers appeared. On the whole, Lithuanians greeted them in a friendly manner since they were happy to be rid of the Communists. However, the Germans soon showed their claws: as they marched along, they requisitioned horses, cars, anything they wanted. But people still thought: better to lose these things than to be ruled by the Soviets. The Soviet army retreated in panic, pursued by Lithuanian partisans who also gathered around important factories and other installations to protect them from destruction. Even in flight, the Russians tried to take along the people they had jailed. If they didn't have enough time, they tortured and shot the prisoners on the spot. Terrible prison massacres took place in the towns of Telšiai, Panevėžys, and Pravieniškiai. Other prisoners, including many priests, were forced into death marches and shot along the way. Fleeing along with the Russians were those local people who had collaborated with them.

Already by the second day of the war, Lithuanian partisans occupied the Kaunas radio station and announced to the country that a temporary Lithuanian government had been formed.

The German Occupation, 1941–44

The German invasion did not bring the freedom that Kazys had hoped for. Disregarding the temporary government that the Lithuanians had formed, the Nazi regime sent a German High Commissioner to administer the newly won territory. Because the Germans didn't speak Lithuanian, they established councils of local people who were obliged to carry out their orders. Lithuanians found themselves under the strict control of the new occupiers and reacted with passive resistance. Young men avoided the military draft, people tried to ignore the many regulations, farmers hid their animals and crops. The Lithuanian police were more likely to warn people to hide than to arrest them. Kazys was constantly hungry since food was rationed and the amounts allotted per person were barely enough to keep people alive. Farmers, and those who had close contacts with farm people, were better off than the townspeople.

Kazys' situation improved when he started to expand the electricity net to surrounding villages. The farmers bribed the German administrators with food products in order to get the needed construction materials. Some of them were so eager for electricity to arrive at their farms that they volunteered to provide some of the labor. When the first light bulbs went on in their homes, the grateful farmers often brought food to town for Kazys and his staff.

The Jews of Lithuania suffered the most under German occupation. Jews had lived in Lithuania since the 8th century serving an important role as traders between the Baltic area and Russian lands. In 1388 the Grand Duke Vytautas issued an invitation to the Jews of Western Europe to settle in Lithuania and a large number of them, fleeing persecution in Western countries, accepted his invitation. Vytautas was eager to bring in people who were skilled in various crafts and trades to raise the standard of living in Lithuania. Pagan Lithuania welcomed the Jews. The grand dukes offered them rights and privileges they did not have in Western Europe. When Lithuania was united with Poland and Christianized, the Catholic Church began to spread anti-Semitic ideas. Nonetheless, Lithuanian Jews lived peacefully for centuries with their Christian neighbors. They developed renowned cultural centers and theological schools (yeshivas). Vilnius was known as the "Jerusalem of the East" for its Jewish scholarship and learning. The Litvaks (Lithuania's Jews) were regarded as the most learned and intellectual among the Jews of Eastern Europe. In the 19th century, under the Czarist regime, Jews in Lithuania's rural villages were as poor as their Christian neighbors. Many of them emigrated to the United States and other parts of the world to escape poverty and service in the Czarist army.

During the first Soviet occupation, a significant number of Jews sided with the Russian invaders either because of their attachment to Communist ideals or because they saw the Russians as a bulwark against the Nazis. Since Lithuanian Jews typically spoke Russian, in addition to Yiddish and Lithuanian, the Soviet authorities recruited them to act as translators and interrogators. Some of them collaborated with the Soviets during the arrests and deportations. As a result, other Lithuanians saw these Jews as traitors and were inclined to generalize the same about the whole Jewish population. When the Germans marched in, they found enough anti-Semitic Lithuanians who were willing to collaborate with them in violence against the Jews. It was unfair to label all Jews as "traitors" and it is equally unfair to blame the brutal actions of those who collaborated with the Nazis on Lithuanians in general. Many Christians risked their lives to save Jews. If caught, they were killed immediately or deported to concentration camps. Jews were rounded up and placed into ghettos. After an uprising, the Jewish quarter of Vilnius was almost completely destroyed. A large massacre of Jews took place in the forest of Paneriai, near Vilnius. Before World War II, 220,000 Jews had lived in Lithuania, about 7% of the population. When the Nazis finished their extermination campaign, 207,000 Lithuanian Jews had been murdered — almost the entire population. This is one of the darkest chapters of Lithuanian history and a great loss to the country.

Chapter 5:
Kazys and Jadvyga Meet and Marry

By the time Kazys finished his studies and was financially independent, he was already 27 years old. Then came the war and the occupations. In such chaotic times, Kazys didn't feel he could think about marriage. Besides, he was quite happy in his well-furnished bachelor pad that looked out on the Šiauliai city park. He had plenty of friends, a good social life, women who liked him. But there was no one around him who was a true soul mate, and often he felt alone and lonely, with no one to share his deeper thoughts and feelings. In May 1942 he traveled to the town of Mažeikiai where he was organizing the delivery of electricity from Latvia. It was here that he saw Jadvyga for the first time. He described the meeting:

Jadvyga and Kazimieras' wedding photo. March 4, 1943.

It was a beautiful Sunday afternoon. I had met up with a childhood friend, a girl from my village named Regina Gavelytė and together we took a walk in the town park. As we were walking, she pointed out in the distance an attractive blond girl who was accompanied by the director of the local bank. Regina told me this was Jadzė Bolytė, a nurse in the Mažeikiai hospital who was living with her brother, a doctor in the town clinic. The Bolis (also called Bolisas) family had lived in Alytus for a long time, so I knew the older brothers. I was curious to meet this girl who had lived near my village. Regina introduced me to Jadzė but we only talked for a short time. Jadzė was beautiful and friendly, perhaps a bit too proud, but that banker companion of hers was quite unpleasant, so I took my leave. Soon after that I left Mažeikiai and had no chance to return that summer, but I didn't forget Jadzė. That fall of 1942 I returned again to Mažeikiai, this time for a longer stay. That's when Jadzė and I began our friendship. I don't know if I was in love with her, but it felt good to be with her, and I wanted to be with her all the time.

Jadzė lived in Mažeikiai with her brother Leonas, a medical doctor, and his wife. They all worked together in the hospital.

By then I was 30 years old, high time to think about marriage. First, I had to make a big decision. Not long before, I had met a fine girl, Vanda, who had just finished secondary school and was about the same age as Jadzė. Vanda had fallen in love with me and was waiting for me to say the word. I had to decide whether to choose Vanda and make her happy or try to win Jadzė to whom my heart was drawn.

I went to a New Year's celebration (1943) where some of my close friends had gathered, including a priest I knew. These friends were aware of my dilemma, so someone suggested we drink a toast to the town of Telšiai (that is, to Vanda). Most everyone raised a glass to Telšiai, except for the priest, who toasted to Mažeikiai (to Jadzė). I too had to make a toast, and though many years have passed since then, I remember clearly how I raised my glass and drank to Mažeikiai. That was the moment of my decision. Soon after that, I traveled to Mažeikiai, went to Jadzė and asked for her hand. Jadzė did not give me a clear answer; she avoided making a decision. I left dejected that my marriage proposal had failed, returned to Šiauliai and vowed to forget Jadzė. But a few days later Jadzė telephoned me to say she was coming to see me in Šiauliai. I met her at the train station as someone for whom I had been waiting a long time, someone *so dear to me. It was a cold Sunday morning; the air was full of snowflakes. But my heart felt warm and at peace. That's when we decided to link our destinies for all time.*

I visited Jadzė in Mažeikiai a few more times. Train connections were difficult in wartime so it was impossible to visit each other often. We decided not to wait much longer but get married before Lent. Jadzė's brother Leonas agreed with that plan. Our pre-marriage friendship was so short, yet it left me with beautiful, unforgettable memories.

Jadvyga and Kazys were married on March 4, 1943, on St. Casimir's Day, our father's patron saint. From brother Leonas' house they walked by foot to a nearby church, accompanied by four witnesses. Due to the scarcities of wartime, they wore simple clothes and even finding gold rings was a major challenge. Kazys experienced the ceremony with deep emotion.

Even though I had fallen away from religion at that time, after the ceremony I knelt at the altar and prayed to God for help to always stay faithful to my wife. [...] When we left the church, it was a beautiful late afternoon. The rays of the setting sun were like a symbolic farewell to my bachelor days. I felt I would not miss them for I was starting a more meaningful life — I now had a faithful friend with whom I would share all sorrows and joys."

Returning to Leonas' home, they found the guests already waiting. Jadvyga's mother met the newlyweds at the door with bread and salt, a Lithuanian tradition that signifies a good life together. Jadvyga's and Leonas' medical friends in Mažeikiai were present at the wedding celebration but family members from other parts of Lithuania were unable to come because of the difficult travel conditions in wartime. The newlyweds returned to Šiauliai that same night, a five-hour train ride. Traveling with them was another couple, friends of Kazys. Our father recalls that the four of them sang the entire way — they were so happy. In Šiauliai they organized a second wedding celebration, inviting Kazys' friends and coworkers, including the priest who had proposed that memorable toast to Mažeikiai.

Their married life started modestly: *At first we had only one room with only the most essential furniture. But we didn't lack for anything.* Soon they rented a pleasant apartment and furnished it comfortably. Then Jadzė invited her mother to come from Mažeikiai to live with them.

Many years later, living in the United States, we asked our mother to share her memories about their courtship. She said: "He was very much in love with me. When he visited he brought me flowers — one time, a pot of pink cyclamen.

We sat and talked in Leonas' house or went to the movies. He was so serious — I was afraid he was too serious for me. I was still so young, wanting to have fun, not thinking about marriage." When she met Kazys, Jadzė was nineteen years old. She did not feel ready for a serious relationship with this older man. Friends of Leonas, a family named Šadauskas, were well-to-do owners of a beer brewery in Mažeikiai. They gave a party to which she and Kazys were invited. She was enjoying herself dancing and flirting with other men, but Kazys became jealous. He pulled her attention back to himself by burning his finger when his lit cigarette came in contact with some spilled whiskey. As a nurse, Jadzė rushed to his aid and bandaged up the finger. Was it an accident? Our mother did not think so. Her other admirer at that time was the bank director. She did not like him much, however, because he was a "womanizer" and seemed unreliable to her.

When Kazys proposed, Jadzė was at a loss what to say. She told him this was too soon, too sudden. As soon as he left, she went to her room, fell on her bed and started to cry. Her sister Stefa came into the room and advised her, "Stop crying and just say no." Jadzė talked to her mother who said that Kazys seemed like a good person. Jadzė agreed and felt he sincerely loved her. She also considered her situation: she, her widowed mother, and her younger sister Stefa were living with her brother Leonas whose wife was not welcoming. Jadzė must have been eager to escape from an uncomfortable situation. Kazys, handsome and with a good profession, was a desirable match. She decided to say "yes." When they married, she was 20 years old; he was almost 11 years older.

Shortly after the newlyweds had settled into their own apartment in Šiauliai, Jadzė found a nursing job at the city hospital and was quickly appointed head nurse. Here she saw first hand the human suffering of war: wounded soldiers of different nationalities, injured partisans, and civilians were brought for treatment. The hospital did not turn anyone away. Their first child was born on January 12, 1944, "a beautiful, healthy girl," according to Kazys. The parents baptized her Audronė Aurelija on March 4, on their first wedding anniversary. The godparents were Vladas Klajumas, father's co-worker, and Regina Snarskienė, the wife of father's boss. Jadzė's mother who had moved from Leonas' home in Mažeikiai to Kazys' and Jadzė's apartment helped care for the baby. Our father remarked about the first year of marriage: "Life was beautiful and meaningful but our happiness did not last long." As the Soviet Army marched toward Lithuania in 1944, the country once again became a battlefield.

Jadvyga's relatives in Lithuania: Photos from World War II and the Soviet Era.

Jadvyga's mother Kotryna with sister Stefa, about 1943.

Aunt Teresė, the sister of Jadvyga' mother.

Stefa (2nd from right at top) and husband Alfonsas Gintendorfas, with daughters Virginija and Alfreda; Alfreda's first Communion.

Stefa and Alfonsas holding daughter Alfreda.

Jadvyga's brother Leonas, his two daughters, Irena and Onutė, his wife Elena; Stefa with daughters Virginija and Alfreda.

Aunt Stefa was a nurse's aide at war's end.

Two Bolis families intermingled. Marcelė, Leonas, Antanas, Elena, Onutė, Stasytė and Irutė.

Jadvyga's brother Antanas with wife Marcelė and daughter Stasytė.

Antanas, son of Jadvyga's brother Feliksas, with his wife and children, Laima and Virgilijus; Kėdainiai.

The family of Jadvyga's sister Stefa. L. to R.: Daughter Virginija, Stefa, her mother-in-law, husband Alfonsas Gintendorfas, daughters Daiva and Alfreda..

Jadvyga's brother Pranas; photo sent from Siberia about 1950.

Jadvyga's brothers Olekas and Leonas with their wives, both named Elena.

Kazys' mother Magdalena with grandson Rimas (Monika's son) in Veiveriai, 1960s.

Kazys' and Jadvygas's relatives meet each other through our visits. Here Kazys' brothers Juozas and Vladas, Jadzė's sister Stefa, Juozas' sister-in-law Vanda, and Monika's daughter Danguolė. 1968.

Kazys' sister Damutė's family. L to r: Elegijus, Valdas, Damutė, Edmundas, husband Antanas, Juozukas and Arvydas. 1980.

Irena Baranauskaitė, daughter of Kazys' brother Juozas, taught herbal medicine at Kaunas University. She visited the USA in 1988.

Kazys' sister Damutė's wedding: Back row: Juozas Atmanavičius (Monika's husband), sister Monika, Kazys; Front: the bride Damutė, groom Antanas, unidentified woman. 1940.

Kazys in His Many Roles

The Engineer. Kazys designed large-scale electrical power plants for the Charles T. Main Company in Boston.

The Builder. Thomas (now Vytas) helps his "Tėvukas" build a greenhouse in Manomet, while Jadvyga watches; 1978.

The Poet. Kazys, in his 80s, recites by heart an epic poem he learned in his youth.

Kazys playing Marley's ghost in a Boston Lithuanian production of "A Christmas Carol."

The Grandfather. Kazys walks on the beach with Algis' daughter Laura, age two. His "lazda" (walking stick) impressed the grandchildren. 1983.

Kazys, the gardener, at Audra's house in 1995.

Chapter VI: Jadvyga's Origin

Our mother Jadvyga (Hedwig) was born on October 5, 1922, in the town of Kėdainiai located about 30 miles north of Kaunas in central Lithuania. Her father, Antanas Bolis (the family name also appears as Bolisas and Bolevičius)[1], was born in Kaunas in 1881 or 1882. His parents, Kazimieras

Jadvyga's Aunt Teresė, mother, Kotryna, brother Aleksandras and father Antanas around 1905.

Bolis and Salomėja Babičaitė Bolienė, originally came from Ariogala, a small town about 20 miles to the east of Kėdainiai. Antanas was a cobbler by trade with the rank of "master." He was qualified to train apprentices in his workshop which was located in the center of Kėdainiai, close to the market where farmers came to buy and sell. Among his apprentices were his own five sons, all of whom learned how to make and repair shoes. Antanas died of a heart attack in 1930, age 48 or 49.

[1] The family name with its variations, Bolis, Bolisas, or Bolevičius, derives from the given (first) name Boleslavas.

Jadvyga's mother Kotryna (Katherine) was born on May 5, 1882, in Kėdainiai. Her parents, Martynas Budrys and Ona Lapinskaitė Budrienė, lived in the district of Kėdainiai where Martynas was the watchman of a forest that belonged to a nobleman's estate. His job was to protect the forest from poaching and illegal woodcutting. We do not know if Jadvyga's parents Antanas and Kotryna met in Kėdainiai or in Kaunas, however we do know that they were married in Kaunas on February 3, 1904. They probably moved to Kėdainiai shortly after that, for it is there that Antanas established his business. The couple had five sons and two daughters who reached adulthood. Left a widow with two young daughters, Kotryna had a difficult life, moving from place to place, struggling to survive. After she moved to Šiauliai to live with Jadzė and Kazys, she remained with them during the flight from Lithuania to Germany. She died in Hanau, Germany, in 1948. I have a few vivid memories of this grandmother that I will share in the chapter on the displaced person camps.

The Seven Bolis Children

Aleksandras (Alexander), nicknamed Olekas, was born in 1904, died in 1972. He learned the cobbler trade from his father, then opened his own workshop and shoe store in Alytus. He married Elena Kunevičiūtė. They had a daughter, Vanda, who became a dentist, and a son, Edvardas, who was a construction engineer. We met Uncle Olekas when Klaus and I visited Lithuania for the first time in 1969. He was a handsome gentleman, with a full head of silver hair, kindly and considerate. He died three years after our visit. However, on future visits I became good friends with his son Edvardas and his family. As mentioned earlier, Edvardas visited us in the United States in 1988. Although Edvardas has died, the relationship with his

Olekas' and Elena's wedding picture.

family continues to this day: with his wife Vytė, daughter Edita Stankevičienė, and grandson Kristupas Baublys.

Feliksas (Felix) was born in 1906. He remained in Kėdainiai and followed in his father's footsteps in the cobbler trade. He had three children: son Antanas and daughters Vanda and Stasė. Our father Kazys mentioned that Feliksas drank more than usual. He also suffered from epilepsy. In a telephone conversation with Aunt Stefa (November 2012) Dana and I heard for the first time about the tragic circumstances of his death. Feliksas liked to fish. One day, while fishing on the shore of the Nevėžis River, he suffered an epileptic seizure, fell headfirst into the river and drowned. He died about 1950 in his forties.

Feliksas with wife Veronika and children Vanda and Antanas.

Antanas (Anthony) was born in 1908. He too became a cobbler but when he married a farmwoman, Marcelė, he took up farming in addition, in the village of Dusmenys near Alytus. He had a son, Antanas, and a daughter, Stasė, who died of tuberculosis as a young woman leaving a small son behind for Uncle Antanas and his wife to raise. Uncle Antanas, a gentle and sensitive man, became depressed and committed suicide in 1986. I remember how shocked our mother Jadzė was when she learned what had happened to one of her favorite brothers.

Kind and gentle Antanas did not drink alcohol.

Pranas (Francis) was born in 1910. Our father mentioned that he had artistic talents but that he continued in the family's cobbler trade. Eventually, he found a job in a prison workshop in Kaunas where he taught shoemaking to the inmates. The Soviets deported him to Siberia in 1945, perhaps because of his employment in the prison. He married a Russian woman in Siberia, had a son, and died in exile in 1955. The son returned once to

Lithuania to find his father's relatives but the visit was not a happy one. He was welcomed at first but when the relatives discovered he was an alcoholic, they stopped supporting him. He returned to Russia.

Leonas (Leo) was born in 1912. He studied medicine at the university in Kaunas and became a medical doctor. He married Elena Osteikaitė, a nurse. Together they had two daughters, Irena and Ona (Ann). He and his family lived in Mažeikiai at first and then moved to Vilnius where he died suddenly of a heart attack in 1970. Our father Kazys remembers him as quiet and slow in manner. Klaus and I met him on our visit in 1969. We were invited to his apartment in Vilnius for dinner, where, to our surprise, we found fish swimming in the bathtub. Since his wife was already dead, our Aunt Stefa was in charge of the meal and she clearly wanted to serve us very fresh fish.

The handsome Pranas died in Siberia.

Jadvyga (Hedwig). Our mother, nicknamed Jadzė, born in 1922, was eighteen years younger than her oldest brother Olekas. Since she lost her father at a young age, Olekas became like a father to her. In the ten-year gap between her birth and that of Leonas, her youngest brother, her mother either had some miscarriages or gave birth to infants who did not survive. Our mother was not sure about these facts because "such things were not discussed with children in those days." About ten years into their marriage, Kazys described Jadzė in his memoir, emphasizing her attractive appearance

Jadvyga — 5 years old.

and pleasant personality: *"It's difficult for me to describe Jadzė objectively because she has become a part of me. She has a fine figure, tall, with blue eyes and blond hair. She has a lovely soprano voice, likes to sing and has artistic talents. She loves children and her nursing profession. She is industrious, organized, and willing to make sacrifices for the welfare of others. She can also be determined and persistent when she sets herself a goal. She is pleasant, friendly, and well liked by people."*

These comments strike me as strangely superficial — they could have been written by anyone who spent ten minutes with our mother. Did our father know her so little? Or was he unwilling to put his deeper thoughts and feelings on paper? I suspect that both of these possibilities may be true.

Top to bottom: Leonas, Pranas, Jadzė and Stefa in 1928.

Stefanija (Stefa) was born in Kėdainiai on March 15, 1926. Close in age to Jadzė, she was also emotionally the closest sibling to our mother. Soon after Jadzė married, Stefa married as well, although she was only 17 or 18. Her husband, Alfonsas (Alphonse) Gintendorfas, was born in Lithuania but was of German origin. The German family name was formerly Hintendorf. Perhaps because of his German heritage, when the Russians invaded, he was deported to Siberia but returned after about five years. The couple lived in Kaunas where Stefa worked in a hospital as a nurses' aid and Alfonsas as an accountant. They had two daughters, Alfreda and Virginia. Alfonsas was a strikingly handsome man but a difficult person. To be honest, Klaus and I found him quite obnoxious. Stefa, a meek and gentle woman, had to put up with his tyrannical nature. Alfonsas' mother lived with them, and she too was demanding and rigid. One of the two daughters, Alfreda, caused Stefa much grief. While still in her teens and unmarried, she gave birth to a daughter, Daiva, whom Stefa and Alfonsas officially adopted and raised. Alfreda became an alcoholic, married an alcoholic, and in a drunken fight, she stabbed her husband to death. Due to extenuating circumstances (self defense), she served only a brief sentence. After Alfonsas died and Stefa became elderly, Alfreda became her caretaker. Our mother, feeling guilty about the good life she was leading in comparison to Stefa's misery, regularly sent her sister money over many years. The relationship between the sisters was a loving and close one, in spite of the great distance between them. Our mother visited Lithuania three times, briefly in 1988 and 1992, and longer in 2000; she was overjoyed to see Stefa after so many years.

Kėdainiai and Alytus

W hile Kazys was the son of farmers, Jadvyga grew up in towns. Farms were an alien world to her — she did not like them. Kėdainiai, on the banks of the Nevėžis River, was a small town in my mother's time (about 7,500 inhabitants). However, it had a long history. First mentioned in a document of 1372, it was a significant center of trade and industry. Leather tanning and shoemaking were among the important crafts. Walking through the streets of town Jadzė would have heard different languages spoken: Polish and Yiddish, along with Lithuanian. Jadzė grew up bilingual, speaking both Polish and Lithuanian. Polish predominated in the towns and cities of Lithuania into the 1920s because the Polish language was associated with the gentry, thus with a higher social status. Lithuanian was considered the "uncultured" language of the peasants. Since about half of the people in Kėdainiai were Jews, Yiddish was heard everywhere. Along with the mix of languages, the town offered a colorful mosaic of different religions and places of worship. Because the Protestant Radvila (Radzivil) family had ruled the area for generations, Kėdainiai became a center of the Protestant Reformation in a sea of Catholicism. The Protestants built an imposing stone church in classical style, while the Catholic one was wooden and more modest. The Jews had several synagogues and Talmudic schools; the Russian Orthodox Christians had their place of worship. This mix of religions and ethnicities was common in Lithuania's cities and towns before World War II. The country has always been a cultural crossroad between Eastern and Western Europe. But in Kėdainiai at that time, the situation was unusual because Catholics there were a minority. Our mother recalled that she enjoyed listening at the doors of the Russian Orthodox church because the chanting was so beautiful. When she passed the synagogue and looked through the open door, she was intrigued by the sight of men wrapped in shawls who rocked back and forth in prayer. The different religions and ethnicities lived side by side peacefully for the most part but they did not mix. On the Sabbath, Jadzė's mother and other Christian women sometimes went to the houses of Jewish neighbors to do the chores that the Orthodox Jews were forbidden to do on that day. They did this not out of friendship but in order to earn some pocket money. Since the 19th century, Kėdainiai has been, and continues to be, a center of cucumber cultivation. Even as a young girl, Jadzė went with her mother to help harvest the cucumbers to earn a little money.

Although her family lived simply, she remembered fondly the summer evenings when her brothers and their friends gathered in the garden behind the house, under a large cherry tree. Her family had musical talent: the brothers sang and played instruments — guitars and balalaikas. Jadzė loved to listen to the songs they sang on those long summer evenings. She and her sister Stefa, three years younger, must have been loved and treated like little princesses by their five older brothers. The brothers teased their little blond sister with the big ribbon in her hair by calling her in Polish "Panna Jadzė" (Miss Jadzė). Soon she started to call herself "Panna Jadzė." This became a family joke. Jadzė's favorite brother was Pranas, "because he stayed close to home and helped his mother." I asked her if her father was strict. She said, "No, he was gentle and

kind. When I played in his workshop he would give me some wooden pegs to nail into a shoe form. He wanted to keep me busy so I would stay close by."

When Jadzė was about eight years old, she moved with her family to the town of Alytus in southern Lithuania, to the same district where Kazys had grown up. This must have been in 1929 or

Wooden church in Kėdainiai, where Jadvyga was baptized.

early in 1930. Jadzė explained the reason for the move by saying that her father drank too much, thus her mother Kotryna wanted to get him away from his drinking buddies. The opportunities to drink were built into his job: When his farmer customers came into town to pick up their custom-made shoes (an expensive item), the satisfied farmers invited the master cobbler to "baptize" the new shoes with them in the pub. Antanas, a sociable man, did not know how to refuse. I surmise that there was probably a financial reason for the move as well: Lithuania's economy, as in the rest of Europe, experienced a crisis in those years. Antanas may have lost his workshop, forcing him to move to Alytus to join his oldest son.

Main Street, Alytus, around 1930.

The oldest brother, Olekas, had settled earlier in Alytus with his wife and children, and had established a large and successful shoe workshop. Later, he opened a store for fancy shoes imported from France and Italy. Another brother, Antanas, also lived in Alytus and operated a small shoe workshop. The parents joined these sons in Alytus, bringing with them Pranas, Leonas, Jadzė and Stefa. Son Feliksas and his wife Veronika also moved to Alytus with the parents but returned to Kėdainiai after some time, where Feliksas continued on his own in the cobbler trade. It seems the couple did not get along well with the rest of the Bolisas family, thus they preferred to live closer to Veronika's mother in Kėdainiai. According to Aunt Stefa, father Antanas rented an apartment for his family on Pulko Street, across from a large park. He went to work in his son Olekas' workshop. This must have been a difficult reversal of roles for father and son. But Kotryna now had more control over her husband's drinking. Except for brother Feliksas, the entire family lived in one town and the brothers could assist their mother in various ways. Brother Antanas, who, according to Aunt Stefa, was very fond of his mother, liked to stop by a bakery on his way home and bring her a bag of buns and pastries.

In December 1930 the family was struck by a tragedy that changed Jadzė's life. Jadzė was sleeping in bed with her father (a common situation when beds were expensive and space tight). In the middle of the night, she was startled awake and frightened — her father sat up and was crying out with pain in his

Jadžė's father's funeral. 1. Elena, wife of Olekas 2. Veronika, wife of Feliksas 3. brother Leonas, 4. brother Antanas, 5. mother Kotryna (widow), 6. sister Stefanija, 7. Jadvyga, 8. brother Pranas, 9. brother Feliksas, 10. aunt Teresė (Kotryna's sister), 11. brother Olekas, 12. Babičas (Kotryna's brother-in-law). Alytus, December 1930.

chest. Kotryna sent Pranas into the night to bring the doctor. By the time he arrived, Antanas had died of a heart attack. He was buried on a cold winter day in the town cemetery of Alytus. After the death of her husband, Kotryna had to provide for two young daughters and a son, Leonas, who was still in high school. With no means of support, she was dependent on the assistance of her older sons.

Kotryna remained in Alytus for a few more years — she and the younger siblings probably moved into the home of Olekas on Seirijai Street. Leonas finished high school in Alytus, then moved to Kaunas to attend medical school on a scholarship. Pranas, who had helped Olekas in the workshop, now moved to Palemonas, a suburb of Kaunas, married, and found a job as instructor in a prison workshop where he taught shoe repairing to the inmates. Stefa started elementary school in Alytus, while Jadžė completed several classes of high school.

The Bolisas family has passed down to their descendants many good traits: they were kindly, gentle, good-natured people with artistic talent, particularly for music. Hard work, perseverance, and a strong sense of obligation were guiding values for them. On the negative side, the family has a history of heart disease and a tendency to alcoholism that shows up in some members of each generation.

Kaunas

About 1933 Kotryna moved to Kaunas with her two girls. Pranas had purchased a small house for them on Kapsu Street in Žaliakalnis, a neighborhood located on a hill above the town center. Aunt Stefa still lives in the same neighborhood (2013), while Jadzė's life's journey took her half way around the globe. When we asked our mother why they left Alytus for Kaunas, she told us it was because there was not enough room with Olekas and his growing family. The house in Kaunas on Kapsu Street was primitive — it had no running water and no sewage system. Kotryna dug a deep hole in the back yard and made a wooden cover for it. Into this hole the family members dumped their night pots. She made a meager living by taking in boarders — girls from the countryside who came to Kaunas to attend school.

For Jadzė, Kaunas was an exciting new world. It was Lithuania's temporary capital (Vilnius had been occupied by Poland) and its largest city. Here were broad avenues, cars, trolleys, elegant stores, restaurants, and movie theaters. She liked to walk around town after school with her friends. But her mother was strict; she expected Jadzė to come home directly to do her chores and her homework. Jadzė attended the most prestigious high school for girls, Aušros Mergaičiu Gimnazija (Dawn High School for Girls), where academic standards were much higher than in Alytus. Besides, her command of Lithuanian was deficient — Polish was the language she spoke better. Jadzė had to struggle to meet these new demands. After completing six years of high school, at age sixteen, she entered nursing school at the Red Cross Hospital in Kaunas. She loved her chosen profession, and although she practiced it for only a few years before fleeing from Lithuania, she often spoke about her love for nursing. Unfortunately, she was not able to continue with nursing after settling in the United States: she did not know English well enough, and, needing to earn money right away, she had to take whatever job she could find.

Nurse Jadvyga. She loved being a nurse and identified herself as such for the rest of her life.

After graduating from nursing school (probably 1940), Jadzė accepted her first position at the hospital in Mažeikiai, a convenient choice, since her brother Leonas, now a medical doctor, already lived there. She, Stefa and their mother left Kaunas behind to live with Leonas. Here, in 1942, the two stories of Kazys and Jadzė began to merge.

Aušros Mergaičių Gimnazija, (Dawn High School for girls) graduating class. Can you pick out Jadvyga? She's the third from the left in the second row from the top. Kaunas, 1938.

Chapter VII: The Flight From Lithuania

In 1944 the German army began to retreat before Allied forces strengthened by America's entry into the war. As the Soviet army pushed west, into Lithuania, and the Germans started to fall back, Lithuanians knew they would be in the line of battle once again. They anticipated a renewed reign of terror under the Communists. People had to decide what to do. Kazys, knowing he would be arrested and either killed outright or deported to Siberia, decided to join the partisan troops in the forests, who were already fighting against the German invaders. He planned to bring his three women, Jadzė, her mother Kotryna, and infant Audronė, to a farm where he thought they would be safe. However, an unexpected visitor changed our family's fate and placed us on the path that ultimately led to the United States. This visitor was Jadzė's cousin Sofija, born Babičaitė.

Zosė wirh second husband and son Petras.

Sofija, called Zosė by all who knew her, was an unusual, independent woman. Tall and strikingly beautiful, she had started to pursue an acting career in Kaunas before the war. Her father's family, the Babičas, was of Serbian or Bosnian origin, or perhaps Turkish. Zosė looked exotic, with raven black hair and dark eyes, a contrast to our mother's Nordic, blond and blue-eyed looks. Zosė's acting career was interrupted when, still unmarried, she became pregnant and gave birth to a son whom she named Petras (Peter). Soon after, she married a man of German origin and during the first Soviet occupation, in 1941, she repatriated with him to Germany. Little Petras took on the last name of his stepfather, Roloff.

In July 1944 Zosė sneaked across the border from Germany into Lithuania, together with Petras. By then she was already a widow. Her husband was drafted into the German army and had perished in the war. She went directly to Kėdainiai in order to bring her father back with her to Germany. He refused, however, saying he was too old and too sickly to leave. He preferred to die in his own country. Zosė then hurried to Šiauliai to see her Aunt Kotryna and cousin Jadzė. During World War I Zosė's family had taken refuge in the Ukraine and were stranded there, starving, while the Bolshevik Revolution raged around them. Because Kotryna sent bread from Lithuania to her sister's family, they were able to survive and return to Lithuania after the war. Zosė now wanted to repay that kindness by helping her aunt and cousin. She convinced Kazys that he could not leave his wife and baby to be killed by the Soviet invaders while he fought with the partisans. Jadzė supported Zosė's plan to leave the country, arguing wisely, that at a time of danger a family must stay together.

Our father described this fateful meeting:

Zosė came to us in Šiauliai and urged us to go with her to Germany. I suggested that she take my family but that I would stay behind. However, Jadzė and her mother refused to leave without me. I had made a commitment to an underground organization to join the guerrilla resistance. Some of the leaders of that organization had themselves already fled the country. Since we had no weapons, remaining behind seemed pointless. Zosė, a German citizen and fluent in the language, quickly obtained all the necessary documents. We transported our furniture and other heavy items to the nearby village of Gankiai and placed them in storage with a farmer. We took some food and some essential clothing. We hoped that the war would be over soon and that we would then return. But when the moment came to leave, I was in despair. I felt like I was having a heart attack — my physical and emotional energy reached a low point.

After a great deal of trouble, we boarded a train and departed. When we crossed the border from Lithuania into Germany at the town of Tilžė [Tilsit in former East Prussia], the sun was almost setting. A few other Lithuanians were traveling with us. Together we sang a song written by Bishop Antanas Baranauskas: "Farewell, Lithuania. How happy I was to live in my own country." Pain gripped my heart even though I hoped to return soon. A sad premonition within me said, "Who knows?" Later we learned that a few days after our departure, the Russians heavily bombed the town of Šiauliai, especially around the railroad station, close to where we had lived. Perhaps it was God's providence that sent Zosė to us to save us from death.

The train to Germany was crowded with frightened refugees seeking to escape the approaching Red Army. There were no seats for our family. However, the ever-resourceful Zosė had acquired a ham from a Lithuanian farmer. Few people could remember what a ham tasted like. It was worth more than money. She offered this precious ham to a conductor, if he could find space for us. His mouth watering, he ordered some people to squeeze together so that we had some room to sit on the long trip to Germany. We were four adults, a young boy and a baby: Kazys, Jadzė, Jadzė's mother Kotryna, Zosė, Zosė's son Petras, and I, baby Audronė. Mother's brother Leonas with his wife and two young daughters had come from Mažeikiai to Šiauliai and had boarded the same train. Through the window they saw that their baggage was still sitting on the platform, not loaded on the baggage car. Realizing that their belongings would be left behind, they jumped off the train and ran back to grab the packages. Just then the overfilled train began to move. They shouted to our family that they would take the train tomorrow. That was the last time Jadzė saw her brother. The train we were on was the last train that reached Germany.

Our train moved slowly on tracks that had been bombed and hastily repaired. It pulled over frequently to allow army trains full of wounded German soldiers to pass. Our mother could see through the windows the young men moaning in pain — blood seeping through the bandages. As a nurse, she wanted to help, but there was nothing she could do. She held me in her arms to keep me safe surrounded by the chaos and horrors of war. When we pulled into the station in Berlin, she was distracted by all the pushing and shoving and by my crying. Holding me and grabbing various bundles, she left her purse behind on the train. It contained one object that was especially precious to her: an amber necklace that our father had given her as a wedding gift. My baby carriage did not get unloaded in Berlin, so everyone assumed it was lost for good. But Zosė put in a claim, and much to everyone's surprise, the carriage reappeared some days later. In Berlin, our parents found thousands of refugees camping in the underground part of the station, seeking protection from the daily bombings. I had become seriously ill with diarrhea and the parents were worried that I could die of dehydration. A group of German women, volunteer members of a Nazi organization, were in the station to help the arriving refugees. Zosė, who spoke German well, took me to one of these women. The woman immediately gave me a medicinal tea that took care of the problem. Our parents who feared the Nazi regime were nonetheless impressed by the concern that these volunteers showed toward a foreign family. They gave us blankets to sleep on in the station that first night.

Next day we continued toward Zosė's home in Gotha, a small city southwest of Berlin, in the state of Thuringia. Gotha had no significant industry and was far enough away from the eastern border. Zosė and our parents hoped to wait out the end of the war there in safety. Along the way, we stopped for a night in Waltershausen, a town close to Gotha. Kazys' best friend Jurgis Gavelis had settled there with his wife before the war. Kazys found his friend depressed by the events of the war, shocked by the bombings. Our father never mentioned this visit in his memoir, probably because the memory was too painful. I learned from our mother that Jurgis Gavelis later committed suicide when he learned that the Soviet Army was marching into Thuringia.

Kazys described our life in Gotha:

After several days of exhausting travel we arrived in Gotha, in Thuringia, because Zosė lived there. She had one room and shared the kitchen with the house owner. We had to sleep on the floor but were grateful for the shelter. By then, American and British bombers had already heavily damaged German cities but nonetheless there was order and discipline. Everyone received ration cards — the small amounts of food were just enough to keep us alive. Everything was in short supply but there was almost no black market. Germans refused to pay more than the official price for a product. After a bombing, special trains arrived with prepared meals and clothing for the victims. Workers had been forcibly brought to Germany from Poland, Russia, and from some Western countries. These workers had to wear special signs on their chests and backs; they were restricted by various rules. Refugees from the Baltic countries were not forced to wear such signs and had no special restrictions. I soon found work according to my profession in a laboratory that tested electrical meters. Our family was assigned two rooms in an apartment. Almost all the packages of food and clothing that we had mailed disappeared along the way, so we were left with just the clothes on our backs. Our biggest challenges were to survive the bombings and to find some additional food. The sirens that warned us of approaching bombers howled day and night. When we heard these sirens, we first grabbed Audrutė, wrapped her in a blanket and then rushed to the basement, where we often sat for hours. After spending a night like that, without any sleep, it was difficult to go to work in the morning.

One day, when I was at work, a large squadron of planes flew over the city and started to bomb it. We had just reached the shelter in the basement, when the electric power plant above us was struck directly by several bombs and completely destroyed. Water started to flow into our shelter — we thought we would drown. Fortunately, before it reached the ceiling, the water drained away through a pipe and we all survived.

We went looking for food in the surrounding farms where we managed to buy some vegetables and fruits. It seems that when food is scare, people develop a huge appetite. We were never as hungry as then. We'd finish eating a plate of vegetables but an hour later we were hungry again. Near us was a large bread bakery. Jadzė got to know a young, friendly salesgirl to whom she gave our ration card for oil and she in turn gave us enough bread.

Not long after that, quite a few Lithuanians arrived in Gotha. Being so far from home, it was a great joy to meet a fellow Lithuanian, even a person we did not know. We felt like brothers. A priest named Voldemaras Cukuras arrived as well — he was both energetic and pleasant. He quickly organized a Lithuanian parish, holding Mass in a partly ruined German Catholic church. All the Lithuanians gathered at Mass, including those who had not attended church before. As we sang Lithuanian hymns, we felt like we were back home again. We all waited eagerly for the end of the war and the end of the hated Nazi regime.

Audronė's first Christmas, Gotha 1944.

In the spring of 1945 the war was coming to an end. The immense Allied air force flew back and forth across Germany, hardly meeting any resistance. Showing no mercy, these planes bombed factories, cities, rail lines, and military depots. The German army tried desperately to resist but in many places the soldiers capitulated en masse when they saw that they were surrounded. The American army occupied the city of Gotha in early May. Before that, we spent one night in the basement because the Americans shelled the city with heavy artillery.

The occupying American soldiers behaved as they wished, without much discipline. One time a drunken soldier pushed his way into our apartment and saw that I was wearing a pair of German army pants that I had gotten from a warehouse. Thinking that I was a German soldier in hiding, he grabbed his pistol and tried to shoot me.

When our mother told this story, she added a few details. The American soldier had seen our father on the street wearing the surplus military pants. He followed him to our apartment and accosted him there with a drawn pistol. Grandmother saved the day. She quickly grabbed me in her arms and stood in front of the American soldier. She shouted to our father, "Get out of here." Father dashed out the door. The soldier hesitated, then cursed and left. Several hours later, our father returned unharmed and was not bothered again.

The American military did not know what to make of the refugees from

Lithuania and the other Baltic states. Because the Russians were their allies in the war, they did not understand why these people had fled. Were they Nazi collaborators or criminals? People who had persecuted and killed Jews? When the Lithuanian refugees tried to explain the cruelty they had experienced under the Soviets, some Americans refused to believe it; they dismissed these reports as propaganda.

Once Hitler's government was overthrown, we foreigners could breathe freely again. We stopped going to work for the Germans. The German army warehouses were opened and we brought home clothing, food, cigarettes, and other needed items. One day I walked out into the countryside to exchange tobacco and cigarettes for food. After a lot of effort, I obtained a small bag of flour. It was a hot day, the walk was long, and so I became extremely fatigued. When I returned home, I felt blood seeping out of my mouth. I went right away to a hospital for refugees. That night, blood erupted from my mouth in a great stream that the doctors could not control for a long time. I thought, "This is the end." I stayed in the hospital for three weeks.

The cause of the bleeding was tuberculosis. This near-death experience led Kazys to pray to God: "Lord, if you let me survive this crisis, I will return to the Church and will be a faithful Catholic for the rest of my life." The Lithuanian priest, Father Cukuras, came to the hospital and brought Kazys communion and anointed him with the last rites. Kazys survived, however, and remained true to the promise he had made in his prayer.

Chapter VIII: Life in the DP Camps

Kazys and Jadvyga were relieved when the war ended and the American army marched into Gotha. However, news spread soon that the American army was about to leave the state of Thuringia, turning it over to the Soviets in exchange for a part of Berlin. The Lithuanians in Gotha decided that they must somehow get out of Thuringia and move further west, into the part of Germany that would be under American administration. Soon after arriving in Gotha, our family had been assigned two rooms in an apartment that belonged to a mother and daughter, both of whom were war widows. These German women had been upset at first, when they were forced to share their apartment with strangers, foreigners even. In time, our parents and the two women became friends. Jadzė was discreet and considerate: she used the common kitchen only after the owners were done; she kept everything clean; she was friendly and helpful. Kazys, with his technical skills, was able to repair whatever broke in the apartment. The women appreciated having a man around who could do some muscle work when needed. When our parents told the German mother and daughter that they must move West because the Soviet Army was coming to Thuringia, the women tried to persuade them to stay. They argued that the Russians would only be there temporarily, nothing bad would happen, the war was over, they would all survive. Our parents, however, thought otherwise. They packed up their belongings and made plans to move again.

We found a German farmer, who, for a good price, was willing to take us out of Thuringia in his horse-drawn wagon. When we crossed the border out of Thuringia we breathed a sigh of relief. We then clambered on to a freight train with our belongings and arrived in the city of Hanau. Here, in former German army barracks, a camp was established for refugees, a so-called displaced person camp. The barracks were in terrible condition. We were given a small room and had started to settle in when we were told that tomorrow we would have to move to a different camp. Next day they brought us to barracks near the town of Wiesbaden. These barracks were in even worse shape than the first ones: they were partly bombed and had been badly mistreated by the foreign workers, by Russians, Yugoslavs, Poles and others, who had been brought here by the Germans as forced labor. Our family was given a small but separate room. Two or more families had to share the large rooms. Thus, on June 23, 1945, we started our life in the displaced person camps, DP camps for short.

After Germany's defeat, many foreign laborers, mostly Russians, Yugoslavs, and some Poles returned to their native lands; some were returned by force. The refugees who remained in Germany were placed under the care of the United Nations Rehabilitation and Relief Association (UNRRA). This organization was founded by American initiative and primarily supported with American money. The admirable goal was to help the victims and countries that had lost so much in the war get back on their feet. Unfortunately, many of the officials were corrupt — they had their own purposes that had nothing to do with the organization's noble goals. The American government had given UNRRA about 4 billion dollars, but much of that sum landed in the pockets of these officials.

The administrators of the DP camps decided to place people of all different nationalities together into the camps. Each national group got it's own separate housing. Each nationality elected a representative to keep order among them and to speak for them with the administration. Other camp service people, such as police, firefighters, workers in the warehouses, were chosen from various nationalities. These people tried to gain advantages for their own national group.... The camps were usually surrounded with barbed wire and guards stood at the gates. Our food was primarily out of cans; for lunch we got soup from a central kitchen. We received some clothing as well.

Living in the camps we felt dehumanized, like beggars living from handouts, because we hardly had anything that belonged to us. The UNRRA officials treated us like superfluous beings without any value. We longed desperately for our own country from which we had no news. We consoled ourselves with the hope that a new war would break out soon between the USA and Communist Russia. We thought that America, having entered the war with calls for freedom, would not allow the communists to hold millions of people enslaved. After many years I see how both naive and logical we were. In the camps we had a lot of time. People used the time in different ways. Some secretly slipped through the fence and went off to exchange cans of food or a piece of clothing for some fresh food or wine. Others played cards or just hung around aimlessly. Yet others took on cultural tasks: they organized schools, choirs, folk dance and theater groups. Organizations that had existed in pre-war Lithuania were reestablished in the camps. There were plenty of well-educated people, so in every larger camp a primary and a secondary school were established as well as various vocational courses for adults. If UNRRA had thought to create camps based on a single nationality, the conditions for establishing such cultural institutions would have been much better. In Wiesbaden a group of Lithuanian engineers started some workshops where we could produce and repair needed items. Engineers of other nationalities joined us. I was in charge of the electrical section.

While we were living in the Wiesbaden camp, our first son, Rimvydas Kazimieras, was born on October 8, 1945. He was a plump, healthy, and quiet

Electricians class at the trade school in Offenbach DP camp in 1947, where Kazys, fourth from left, was an instructor.

boy. He slept most of the time. The Reverend Paukštys baptized him in the camp chapel. His godparents were Dr. Juodėnas and Mrs. Norkienė.

Wiesbaden had been a resort with world-famous mineral springs known for their healing powers. The lovely countryside was surrounded by forest-covered hills and the Rhine River flowed nearby. Germany's most beautiful river, the Rhine, was praised in songs and legends. The river had carved its way through steep cliffs making it a strategic waterway in the Middle Ages. Its banks are crowned on both sides with medieval castles that look proud and invincible on the high cliffs. The banks along the river are covered with vineyards.

As I raced down the long corridor of our barrack, I had to look carefully not to miss our room. All the doors looked alike. Most were closed, but when a door stood ajar, I peeked inside, curious to see what was there. Usually, I saw only the big blankets that families had hung from ropes to divide a large room into sections for privacy. I could hear voices behind the blankets, talking quietly or arguing. Sometimes children scampered out from behind the blankets and stared at me. Our door was partly open and there was baby Rimas sleeping on the bottom part of a bunk bed, with mother sitting beside him. He was a boring brother, I decided, not at all what I had expected. He'd cry a little, nurse greedily and then fall asleep again. I saw it wasn't time for lunch yet. Father and močiutė (my grandmother) had gone out with empty coffee tins in hand to bring back soup from the large kitchen at the far end of the camp. I knew what kind of soup they would bring — it would be a watery, salty, onion soup, with the few pieces of onion floating around wanting to be caught. That, and a piece of black bread, would be our lunch. They weren't back, so I still had time to play. I skipped off before mother could say anything, ran out the front door of the barrack and called out to my

friend: "Silvia, where are you?" She was a bit older than me, four, while I was almost three. But she was my best friend. When we played in the bushes that grew around the barracks, no one could see us. We could hide as long as we wished. But Silvia was not there now…perhaps she was already in her room eating the onion soup that made us burp and fart.

Celebrating Pentecost at the DP camp in Offenbach. Audra wears a big bow, with Jadzė and Kazys behind her holding Rimas.

In November 1946, when Rimas was just one year old, we were moved to another camp. The American air force took over the Wiesbaden barracks so the refugees had to leave. Our family was sent to Offenbach am Main, a town just east of Frankfurt, because the workshop where Kazys worked was relocated there. A technical trade school was established as well, to which young refugees of various nationalities came from all over the American zone to learn a trade. Our father was in charge of the electrical labs and taught the classes. He noted that the course of study lasted three months then came a new group of students. The DP camp was located about 2 km south of the town of Offenbach, on the Main River. The camp was not large, just a few barracks and buildings. Not counting the students, about 150 refugees lived here. The surroundings were beautiful here too. A pine forest grew nearby and a small creek flowed through the middle of the camp. When our Rimvydas was about two-years-old, he fell into that creek and almost drowned. An older girl pulled him out.

We were playing by the creek when Rimvydas slipped and fell into the water face first. He was wearing a thick winter coat that became soaked with water and made him heavy, too heavy for me to lift him up. He kicked his feet, splashed with his hands, but couldn't get his face out of the water. I was not much older, not yet four — I stood by the creek and cried. An older girl playing nearby heard me and ran over. Luckily, she knew what to do. She didn't try to lift him, like I had. She pulled him sideways until his face emerged from the water. He lay on the ground a while longer, frightened and crying. Finally, together we managed to help him to his feet and walk him home. Our horrified mother pulled off his wet coat, changed him into dry clothes. She had been nursing the newborn twins, Danutė and Algis, and caring for her sick mother. Our father was busy teaching in the technical school. So Rimvydas and I were allowed to roam the camp at will and play wherever we wanted. The camp was fenced, other adults were around; mother thought we would be safe. I had

Rimvydas and Audronė in Offenbach.

been in charge of Rimvydas who had just learned to walk — I knew how badly I had failed him and my parents.

Offenbach was the camp where we stayed the longest, from November 11, 1946 to February 29, 1948. One of my most vivid memories from this camp is the arrival of the twins, Algis and Danutė. Father took me to the hospital to see mother and my new sister and brother. I was terribly disappointed and angry when told that I could not enter the hospital; I was too young. Father and I stood on the lawn facing a large hospital window. Soon my mother appeared with a baby in her arms. A nurse stood next to her holding the other baby. Both babies had their mouths wide open, their faces scarlet; I could hear them screaming through the window. Father looked at me and asked if I wanted to bring these babies home. I said very definitely "No!" He laughed. A week later, a jeep drove up to our house at the camp. My mother sat in the back seat with a large pillow on her lap. On that pillow lay the two babies. I knew they were here to stay. Father recorded this event in his memoir:

While living in the Offenbach camp our twins, Algis and Danutė, were born on August 31, 1947. Both were healthy and beautiful babies. Rev. Bukauskas came from the DP camp in Hanau to baptize them at home.

Algis' godfather was Mr. Kazys Bačiauskas and his godmother was Dr. Marija Svotelienė, while Danutė's godparents were Mr. Rėkus and Marija Šimonienė. All of these godparents now live in America. The conditions of camp living made it difficult to raise the four little ones. We lived in a house next to the camp where we had two rooms for the seven of us. Both twins slept in one carriage, so if one started to cry the other woke up and began to cry as well. Algis had a particularly loud voice.

Jadvyga holds the twins, Dana and Algis, spring 1948.

It was my privilege to wheel the babies around in their carriage. My friends wanted to take a turn at it, but I would not let them. These were MY twins, even if they were difficult to manage. When Algis dropped his pacifier, he would yank the one out of Dana's mouth. Then she started to cry and it was my job to find the other pacifier and stick it into her mouth. Dana and Algis had their cribs facing each other with a doorway in between. They stood at the ends of their beds, looking at each other, holding on to the railings and jumping up and down, their diapers drooping, Diapers hung everywhere in the room on ropes that father had stretched from wall to wall. I was well beyond the diaper stage but the other three needed them. Diaper memories: I wake up in the night and see father standing by the stove, stirring two large pots with diapers boiling in them. Mother has diapers in a basket and is hanging them up to dry.

Life in the camp was not gloomy for me — I didn't even know it was difficult. My friends and I played in the bombed-out ruins of a building. The bricks in the rubble were like giant legos — we constructed houses, bridges, roads with them. Then we transplanted weeds to make our own "gardens." We hardly had any toys nor did we miss them. Sometimes we stood at the chain-link fence that surrounded the camp and observed the world outside, the trucks and pedestrians who came by. German children looked at us and we looked back at them. Sometimes they taunted us: "Ausländer, Ausländer! (foreigners, foreigners!)" But we knew how to get their goat. We yelled in chorus, mimicking the German national anthem: „Deutschland, Deutschland über alles. Zwei Kartoffel, das ist alles. (Germany, Germany above all else. Two potatoes is all you have.).

Christmas in the camp — we have a tree with real candles, decorated with silver tinsel. A real Santa comes to our house carrying a stick in case I've been bad. But no, I tell him I have been a good girl, so he opens his bag and pulls out a gift for me. How did our parents manage to do this — to create a „normal" life for their children in a refugee camp?

Getting enough food was a constant challenge. Our food rations were meager and limited, so we were always hungry. Our father described his efforts to feed the family:

A different organization took charge of the refugee camps. UNRRA was abolished and in its place stepped IRO (International Refugee Organization). IRO had less funding, so our food situation worsened. But the refugees started to find their own solutions: they constructed wooden sheds and started to raise pigs, rabbits, hens to provide themselves with meat. Since the farmers in the area did not have much themselves, it was hard to obtain feed for these animals. To buy some grain or potatoes, I took the train to Bavaria, about 300 km. The railways had been largely destroyed in the war, thus there were few trains. I had to force my way to get into a train, then stand like a sardine in a can for about ten hours. But even in Bavaria, where the farmland is good and the farmers more prosperous, it was difficult to get anything. German money had no value; no one wanted to take it. I had to bring objects such as clothing, shoes, coffee, or cigarettes as exchange items for the animal feed. Then piling my purchases into a handcart I found my way back to a train station where I gave some cigarettes to the station chief so he would send those bags of grain and potatoes to Offenbach. It's hard to imagine now that we had to go through so much effort to obtain such simple products, grain and potatoes, but then it seemed natural. And if we succeeded, we came home cheerful and satisfied.

Now and then the camp authorities distributed packages to each family that had been sent by the Care organization and made possible by generous Americans who had con-tributed to that charity. We

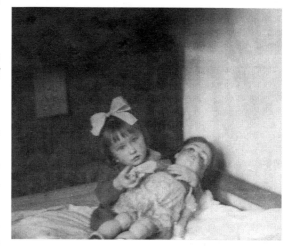

Audra with a doll her size, not hers, at the DP camp.

found all kinds of exciting goods in those packages: there was coffee, cigarettes, candy, sugar, dry beans, rice, cans of Crisco, and much more. When toothpaste and toothbrushes were included, our parents laughed and said we didn't have enough between our teeth to need them. Our father used some of these goods, especially the cigarettes and coffee, to barter with the German farmers for the potatoes we needed. When the first Care package arrived, the statement written on the outside box puzzled our parents: GIFT from the people of the United States. The problem was that „Gift" in German meant poison. What were they to make of that?

I was old enough to have responsibilities. Every day I collected armfuls of grass and throw them into the cages where our few rabbits lived. A communal pig, larger than I, roamed in our yard and wanted to terrorize me. I was terribly afraid of this huge pig. One day it pinned me to the wall, while I screamed for help. In the summer, mother took us into the woods and fields to find sorrel and berries — much needed vitamins for our diet. Grandmother Kotryna, weak and ill, usually stayed behind sitting in her chair in the corner of the room.

Grandmother had wavy silver and black hair that she wore in a bun. She seemed old and strict to me, although I know now that she was only about 65-years-old. One day, ready to go berry picking, I picked up my favorite metal cup to collect the berries. Grandmother told me to leave the cup at home or I would lose it. In my stubborn way I insisted on taking the cup — and sure enough, grandmother was right. I set it down on the ground among the bushes and could not find it.

Kazys and Jadvyga with the four children: Audronė, Algis, Danutė and Rimvydas, in the DP camp in Offenbach.

Mother helped me look, but to no avail. I was miserable over the loss but knew it was my own fault.

The apple peel episode shows how hungry I was for fresh fruit. One evening, standing outside the camp's administration building, I watched several people come out — the people who ran our camp. One of the men was peeling an apple with a small knife. The peel was a perfect spiral hanging down from the apple. When he finished, he let the peel drop to the ground. I had never tasted an apple but had seen them and knew what they were. When the people walked away, I stood for a moment debating what to do. Then I rushed over and picked up the peel. It was delicious! My first taste of apple! How could anyone throw away something so good?

We have a few small, black and white photos that show our family enjoying a Sunday afternoon outing into nature with other Lithuanians. Jadvyga, young and beautiful, is surrounded by her four children. Algis and Dana are still babies in her arms, while Rimvydas and I can stand on our own feet. We look healthy but our tall father is just skin and bones — he looks almost like a concentration camp inmate. I think our parents gave us children most of the food they had, keeping little for themselves.

On March 1, 1948, our family was transferred to the larger DP camp in nearby Hanau, 25 km east of Frankfurt am Main. We lived here for a year-and-a-half. Riding the streetcar into the center of Hanau, I saw scenes of terrible destruction. The streets were lined with rubble and the remaining bombed out buildings looked like they were about to topple. In the middle of the central square, where the ruined city hall stood, I could hardly believe my eyes — there

was a beautiful bronze sculpture of two men, one standing and the other sitting, both looking at a book. Who were these men? My mother told me they were famous people who had been born in Hanau — the brothers Grimm, Jacob and Wilhelm. I knew the Grimm fairy tales; they were my favorite bedtime stories, read to me by mother in Lithuanian. I stared at the Grimm brothers and was so glad they had survived the war.

Jadvyga, with friends, the Šimoniai, takes a trolley to church in Offenbach.

I remember just one trip into Frankfurt, also by trolley. Our parents took us to the zoo — what an adventure! There were the animals I had seen only in books, greenhouses with tall palms and the smell of tropical plants. Even yellow bananas hung from a tree! Before we left, mother bought me a small banana, so ripe that it was almost black. It was the most delicious thing I had ever eaten. On our way home, while walking through a park, I noticed a five-mark bill lying under a bench. Our parents, with Rimvydas,

Danutė, and Algis in hand, were ahead of me on the path. I rushed over to them waving the five-mark bill and gave it to my mother. She asked if no one had been around who might have lost the money. I said, no. This seemed to me like a lot of money and I was sure our parents would use it to buy some food or some clothes we needed. Instead, a few days later, mother presented me with my first doll, a little thing with a pretty face and painted blond hair. She had used the 5 marks to buy it for me. I was thrilled. Our parents tried to create a normal life for us children under difficult conditions. This never ceases to amaze me.

Our grandmother, Kotryna, became seriously ill in the Hanau camp and was taken to the city hospital. I visited her there once and watched as our mother looked after her, brought her food from home, helped her drink, trimmed her toe nails. No one told me at the time that grandmother was dying of intestinal cancer. Our mother visited her every day in the hospital until she died on April 13, 1948. Mother's friends in the camp prepared grandmother Kotryna for burial, placed her in a coffin that stood in a garage-like room with the large door open, so all the camp's Lithuanians could gather outside. Our mother went up to the coffin, said something quietly to her mother — perhaps words of farewell — and then reached down to lovingly close her mother's eyes. She then motioned for me to come closer to the coffin to bid grandmother goodbye. I shook my head and moved away; my first sight of a dead body frightened me. At the burial I had no choice: along with everyone else, I had to take some dirt in a small shovel and throw it on the coffin that had been lowered into the grave. The sound of the dirt falling on the coffin rang in my ears for days. I was sad and shocked to lose my grandmother.

Jadvyga lost her mother when she was 25. Kotryna is buried in Hanau, Germany.

In a corner of the Hanau cemetery reserved for foreigners Kotryna was laid to rest, along with other refugees whom the war had driven far from their homes. Our parents erected an imposing black cross on her grave and inscribed the words: "Miegok ramiai, brangi mamyte." (Sleep peacefully, beloved mother). I visited Kotryna's grave on my first trip back to Germany in the 1960s. Dana brought the parents there when they visited her in Munich in 1978. Many years later, while staying in Germany, Klaus, Vytas, and I again made a trip to Hanau to visit the cemetery and Kotryna's grave.

The Lithuanian refugees, with tongue-in-cheek humor, transformed the initials DP into "Dievo paukšteliai" (God's little birds) and like little birds, they all wanted to fly far away from the camps. Father recalled how tired people were of living in the camps:

Life in the camps became unbearable after some years. No one wanted to remain in Germany, since no one believed that Germany would be able to rebuild and return to normal life in the near future. We all wanted to emigrate — no matter where, even to hell — just to get out of Germany. The truth is, we did not feel safe in Germany. The Russian government considered us its citizens and made efforts to get us back. We were afraid that the Allies might turn us over to the Russians. At this time, representatives from various countries began to appear in the camps to recruit cheap labor. They selected only the individuals who were fit for specific kinds of work; their families were not included. Many young men went to the coalmines in Belgium and ended up in very difficult and primitive working conditions. England accepted a limited number of people whom they needed for agricultural work. Then the exodus started to Canada, but they took only young, single men for work as lumberjacks in the forests and unmarried women to work in hospitals or as domestic help. Australia was probably the first country to take entire families; so many refugees chose to go there. But most eyes were focused on America (the United States). Whoever had relatives or friends there made efforts to go to America. They hoped to receive an invitation with a guarantee of a place to work and a place to live. Our relatives in America and Canada were not inclined to help us, so we signed up to go to Australia.

Entry into the United States became easier after Congress passed the Displaced Person Act in June 1948, that opened up the doors to many more refugees. However, those wanting to come to the United States still needed a sponsor who was a US citizen and who could guarantee assistance with a place to live and a job. Americans did not want the new immigrants to become welfare cases. Many more Lithuanians with families, who until then were stuck in the camps, now had hope of a better future.

One Sunday, while visiting the nearby Hanau camp, I unexpectedly met

Mrs. Mėlynienė. She told me that her family was getting ready to travel to America. They had obtained the necessary documents with the help of our acquaintance, Professor Simas Sužiedelis, who had left the DP camps earlier. He had found a kind Lithuanian woman born in the United States, who signed the guarantee for a place to work and to live. Mrs. Mėlynienė suggested that I write to Professor Sužiedelis. I did that immediately. After some time I received a reply from him saying that the same woman was willing to sponsor us as well. This woman is Miss Julija Jakavonytė (Yakavonis) who lives in Brockton, Massachusetts. Her parents had immigrated to America from the region of Dzūkija, I think from the village of Marcinkonys. She herself was born in America but spoke Lithuanian fluently and identified herself as Lithuanian. She is also a pious Catholic. She graduated from college in legal studies and has worked for many years as an assessor for Brockton's city government. She is an intelligent and cultured woman. Once we filled out the necessary documents, we started to prepare for emigration to the United States.

People wanting to immigrate to the United States had to pass before all kinds of interview committees that checked on our health and our political views. They were especially concerned about the health of our lungs and eyes. If there was any suspicion that a person had TB or an infectious eye disease, that individual was denied entry. I had been infected with TB earlier, so there were signs of the disease (calcium deposits) in my lungs, but I got through all the examining committees successfully. My wife and children were all healthy.

Years later, mother told me how Kazys avoided being disqualified for the traces of TB in his lungs: he obtained a lung x-ray from a healthy Lithuanian friend and switched it with his own. In this way, he managed to fool the health commission into passing him. Some years after we were already living in Savin Hill (Boston), an x-ray of his lungs showed some active spots of TB. The health authorities wanted to send him away to a sanatorium for six months. Kazys, however, argued that he could not stop working and could not leave his family. We would not be able to survive without his salary. The doctors allowed him to live at home and be monitored regularly. I remember the many bottles of calcium pills that stood in our kitchen pantry. Father swallowed handfuls of these pills several times a day. After about a year, he was declared cured. We children also had to be tested regularly for TB. It was scary to go to the sanatorium in Roxbury and have people in white coats poke needles into the skin on our arms to see if we developed a reaction to some medication. Luckily, we never did.

On September 21, 1949, we were transferred from the Hanau camp to temporary quarters in Butzbach, then on to Grohno near Bremerhaven where we stayed only about eight days. On October14, 1949 we boarded the boat *USS General S. D. Sturgis*. Father remembers it was three in the afternoon when we set sail for the United States from the harbor at Bremerhaven.

Jadvyga's cousin Zosė, our savior who led us out of Lithuania in 1944, had already left Germany a few years earlier. Soon after finding herself in a DP camp in the American zone, she met and married a Polish man. When the camp authorities urged refugees to return to their home countries, Zosė's husband decided to go back to Poland. Zosė and her son Peter went with him. Only much later, after settling in the United States, our parents learned what had become of her. Her Polish husband had died after about ten years of marriage and Zosė found herself alone in Poland. With no chance of emigrating west, she decided to return to Lithuania. Her son Petras, a young man by then, went with her. She lived in Kaunas, in the same neighborhood where she had lived before leaving for Germany. Klaus and I met her on several visits to Lithuania, as did our parents in 1988. What an amazing irony of fate: through her initiative we escaped the Soviets and reached America, while she returned to live under Soviet rule (which she hated) to the end of her life. After she died, her son Petras told Dana that she had been a leader in the underground resistance movement for many years but had to keep it secret, even from us.

Chapter IX: First Steps in America

Kazys' passport photo shows that he had lost a lot of weight in the DP camps.

In Chapter One I described my memories of the difficult trip across the Atlantic Ocean on the "General Sturgis." Kazys reflected on what this voyage meant to him:

As we moved away from the harbor and saw the shores receding in the distance, I felt sad to be leaving old Europe. At first the weather was calm, so sailing was pleasant. But when we passed England's coast and entered the open ocean, a strong wind arose and our troubles started. 'General Sturgis' was not a large ship; it was built for military transport thus not designed for comfort. The women and children were placed in cabins, while the men slept at the bottom of the boat, twenty or thirty to a large room, in cots hanging three one above the other. The powerful wind threw our boat around like a piece of bark. Not accustomed to sailing on the seas, we all became sick. I did not want to eat anything, and if I tried to swallow something, it came right back up. I had no energy, just wanted to sit on the deck, where the fresh air felt good, but we didn't have that privilege. Since we were all still DPs and the transportation was free, we had to work our way across. The UNRRA leaders, who accompanied us, pushed us to do various kinds of work, although we could barely stand up on our legs. Jadzė also had her problems with the four small children whom she had to take to the dining room and try to feed. When the emergency drill alarm sounded at night, she had to put life vests on them and get them up to the deck as quickly as possible. The storm raged on and we suffered through most of our journey. I think even Columbus could not have been

Jadvyga's passport photo.

happier than we were, when we spotted the lights of New York. This was October 25, 1949, the twelfth day of our trip.

We stepped on shore at eight in the morning and were met by representatives of the National Catholic Welfare Conference, Lithuanians born in the United States who drove us to the train station. By train we came to Boston where Reverend Aloyzas Klimas and Mrs. Sužiedelienė met us at the station and drove us to Brockton. Mr. and Mrs. Sužiedelis had a large family (five children) but they took us in and shared whatever food they had.

Audronė's passport photo.

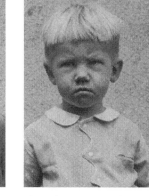
Rimvydas' passport photo.

My first impressions of America: streets full of cars, all sorts of advertisements, the stores full of goods and food products. All this showed me the wealth of the country. However, the dirty streets full of trash showed me that the inhabitants of this country are not much concerned about cleanliness and order.

Algis' passport photo.

Danutė's passport photo.

At the time we arrived, the United States was in the midst of an economic downturn. It was difficult to find work and an apartment. After three days with the Sužiedelis family, we found an apartment consisting of one small room and a tiny kitchen for which we had to pay $12.50 a week. Moving over our few belongings, we started our independent life in this new land. This beginning was truly difficult. It took me three weeks of hard searching before I finally found work in a leather tanning factory. I think my pay was $0.64 an hour. I was unfamiliar with this type of work, it was physically strenuous, but I worked conscientiously and soon earned the reputation of being a good worker. At that time, it was impossible for me to find work in my own profession. I continued to work in that leather factory for about a year and would have worked longer. However, I developed ruptures on both sides of my abdomen that required an operation. Jadzė found a part time job in a small factory that produced leather products.

When the Korean War started in 1950, more opportunities for work opened

First winter in Brockton in clothes donated by a charity. Dana was so thrilled to have a fur coat.

up. After my release from the hospital, I did not return to the factory but found a job in Boston with the Badger Engineering Company. I started to work there on January 4, 1951, as a draftsman on an oil refinery project. At first I did not understand much. This type of work was new for me and I did not understand much English. However, I picked up the work quickly and was promoted to senior draftsman. My first earnings were $1.75 per hour.

Since the daily train ride from Brockton to Boston was inconvenient, I looked for a place to live in Boston. However, no one wanted to rent an apartment, even a miserable one, to a family with four children. There was no way around it — we had to buy a house. With our limited resources we bought an old, run-down house in South Boston at 23 Vinton Street and moved there in August 1951. We did a great deal of work to make the house suitable for living. But as the children grew older, we did not have enough space and the location was not good. We started to look for a better house in a nicer neighborhood.

When I think back to those first five years in the United States, in Brockton and in South Boston, I believe the biggest challenge for our parents was not so much the hard work — they knew how to do that, or the poverty — they had grown up poor, but the shock of an unfamiliar culture and language. Kazys had started to learn English on his own, while still in Germany, then was able to improve his English skills when he started to work as an electrical engineer. Jadzė, however, had great difficulty with English and remained insecure with it all of her life, even after sixty years in the United States. Because of her strong accent, even in old age, people would ask her, "Where are you from." She would answer, "I'm from Lithuania." It was quite funny because those people most likely thought she had just gotten off the boat. Since I immediately started first grade in Brockton, joining the class in the middle of the year, I learned English rapidly. My report card for that year showed my progress: for the first grading period I received all Ds and Fs; in the next grading period my grades were Bs and Cs; finally all As and Bs. It's strange that my teacher gave me any grades at all while I still did not speak or understand English — but that's how

it was at that time. Immigrants were forced to adapt quickly. When someone knocked on the door of our apartment, mother would push me ahead of her to answer the door. She expected me to translate for her and the visitor. This situation frightened me — for a six-year-old it felt like a huge responsibility to mediate conversation between two adults about things she did not understand.

First grade in Brockton was not a happy place for me. My teacher, Mrs. Tuwig, was kind, but the school principal disliked me and took every opportunity to scold me when, with my limited English, I did not understand what I was supposed to do. She even called in our mother for a conference to complain about me: I was a bad girl, didn't obey instructions. Mother knew enough English to understand the

First year in the US — Brockton, MA.

word "bad." She vigorously shook her head: "No, Audronė not bad girl. She good girl." The principal didn't get very far with our mother who refused to accept "bad." In later years, I realized the principal probably thought I was German. I had come from Germany and sometimes said things in German.

So soon after the war there was much hatred in the United States toward all things German. Many people had lost friends and relatives in the war. Who knows what losses the principal had suffered but unfortunately she took her anger out on me.

It's amusing to remember some of the things that happened because our parents were so unfamiliar with American culture and laws. When mother started to work part time, a teenage Lithuanian girl who lived nearby sometimes stayed with us children. Often, mother left me in charge — a six-year-old supervising the three younger ones, ages five and three. The twins were docile but Rimvydas was unruly and hard to manage. He probably resented our parents telling him he must obey his older sister who was not much older than he was. I'm sure our mother was reluctant to leave us alone but felt she had no choice, especially after father developed abdominal ruptures and had to stop working at the factory. Somehow they had to pay for food, rent, and utilities. They were too proud to ask anyone for help. Our parents surely didn't realize they could have been arrested for child endangerment. One time, when mother rushed back from work to prepare dinner and take care of the little ones, she sent me on an errand. She handed me a dollar bill and asked me to go to a nearby tavern and buy a bottle of beer, so daddy could have a treat when he came back from work. I walked through the open door of the tavern and up to the bar where half a dozen men were sitting and talking. I reached my hand up to the counter and placed the dollar there, then asked for a bottle of beer. The men looked down at this small girl with long braids and almost fell off their stools laughing. "I can't sell you beer. You're too young," explained the bartender grinning from ear to ear. "My mother sent me. It's for my father," I pleaded. "Then she'll have to come herself," he replied. On my way home I cried. I did not understand what I had done wrong? Why would he not sell the beer to me? In Germany, young children often went to the tavern with a small pail in which they brought home draught beer for their parents. I thought mother would scold me for my failure but she only shrugged her shoulders.

It took a long time for mother to heal from the trauma that she had experienced during the war, to feel safe again. When she heard low-flying planes, I remember that she would drop what she was doing and run to the window to see whether "enemy" bombers were approaching.

Looking out the window of our Brockton apartment, I could see railroad tracks crisscrossing a large field, with train wagons standing on the sidetracks — perhaps it was some kind of depot. The four of us often played outside unsupervised — I was nominally "in charge." Although we were forbidden to go there, the railroad yard was a natural draw, especially for the boys. One day, Rimas and Algis went to the train depot with the young boy who lived downstairs. They climbed up into a train wagon and were playing around when a security guard caught sight of them and came running. I stood below, calling them to come down. The boys quickly threw some bags of lime fertilizer on the ground, so they wouldn't have so far to jump. The neighbor boy jumped first, landed on the bags and ran away. Then Rimas jumped, and when he did, the bag burst open. Algis, jumping last, fell into the powdered lime that flew up into his eyes, nose, and mouth. We raced home with him while he cried all the way. When Dana opened the door and saw Algis looking like a ghost, all covered in white powder, she started to laugh. Mother told Dana to be quiet as she cleaned the lime out of his eyes and mouth. When our father came home and our worried mother told him what had happened, he spanked the three of us for disobeying the order to stay away from the train tracks. This was the only time father spanked me. I don't remember that it hurt, but it was humiliating. My pride hurt very much indeed.

Mother asked me to put a sign in our second-floor apartment window — sometimes it said ICE, sometimes MILK. The man who brought the ice walked up the stairs holding a large block of ice on his shoulder with metal pincers. He put the ice into our ice chest — that was our "refrigerator." When the milkman drove by and saw our sign, he placed the bottles of milk by the downstairs door and picked up the empty bottles mother had carefully washed. These were great conveniences, compared to life in the camps. Mother was delighted when they finally bought a washing machine. It was green and yellow and electric! Mother filled the machine with a hose from the kitchen sink. Then the machine swirled and scrubbed the clothes all by itself. It even pumped out the used water through the same hose back into the sink. On top of the machine was a clothes wringer, two rollers that mother turned with a crank. She let me feed the clothes through the wringer and they came out almost dry, ready to hang on the clothesline. Such a welcome work-saver for mother, after all the years spent washing clothes and diapers by hand!

Standing in front of our first house on Vinton Street in South Boston.

Mother had not seen the house in South Boston before father bought it. The day we moved in, she first sat down and cried when she saw how filthy it was. Then she stared to clean the kitchen and kill the cockroaches as she found them. It took her months to get rid of those vermin. Our apartment was on the second floor. Below and above us were renters. At each stair landing there was a tiny toilet with a small window, a water tank above and a chain to pull for flushing. Our toilet stank until mother scrubbed it. There was no shower, no bath in the house. Once a week, mother heated water on the stove and half-filled a metal tub in the kitchen. I got my bath first, then Rimas, while the twins went giggling into the tub together. As soon as he could, father installed a bathtub and a hot water heater in the basement for our use.

Our neighbor, Mr. Strazdas, had a car and would take us on outings. Here we were on our way to Marianapolis, a Lithuanian monestery in Connecticut in 1952.

In addition to the kitchen, we had three rooms, a big improvement over the Brockton quarters. Toward the street was a living room with a foldout sofa where our parents slept and a small bedroom that Dana and I shared. Next to the kitchen, facing the backyard was another bedroom shared by the boys. In the three years we spent in that house, our father never stopped renovating — there was so much to do. He repainted the exterior and interior, repaired the rotten window frames, built a new fence around the yard, and put in a small vegetable garden, while mother planted flowers. Like "magic" the house was transformed, while around us was mostly a slum.

The four of us walked hand in hand through this slum on our daily walk to school and back. It seemed to me a long way; it was at least a mile, and it took us about thirty minutes. I loved this new grammar school — it belonged to the Lithuanian Catholic St. Peter's parish in South Boston. The nuns who taught us, the Sisters of Jesus Crucified, were born in the United States but most knew how to speak some Lithuanian. They were kind and welcoming to us new arrivals; they understood the challenges we faced. Among the children were other refugee boys and girls who had recently arrived from DP camps in

Germany. We made friends right away. My second grade teacher decided after a few days that I could read well enough and could do more challenging work, so she transferred me to third grade. Several times a year, a woman severely crippled by polio, dragged herself on crutches into our classroom. Her arrival was a marvelous event. She brought with her a pile of books from the local public library and began to tell us stories. Just when a story became fascinating, she stopped and said to us: "If you want to know how it ends, come to the library and borrow this book." And borrow I did! I carried home the maximum number of books allowed and raced through them. When father came to turn out the light in our bedroom, I continued to read with a flashlight under the blankets. Caught in the act I was scolded and told I would ruin my eyes. Sure enough, by age eleven I needed glasses. But who cares: books were a wonderful escape from the ugly realities around me, a promise of other, more beautiful worlds. I learned English from reading, even if I made up some of the pronunciations for unfamiliar words.

Dana, clutching dolls, in front of the small vegetable garden Kazys had planted in the Vinton Street back yard.

Walking home from school in the afternoons, we passed smelly bars where men sat around drinking and laughing loudly. We cautiously crossed busy streets. Alone at home we were supposed to do our homework but Rimas often went out to play on the streets with neighborhood boys. My authority did not reach far enough to control him. When mother rushed home from work with grocery bags in her arms, she immediately set about making supper. She wanted it to be ready and hot when father returned from his work in downtown Boston. Through other Lithuanian women, mother had found a job in South Boston at a clothing factory. She did "piecework," fast-paced sewing for which she was paid by the piece. When I visited her there a few times, I saw dust swirling in the air, blown around by a huge fan. Thick layers of dust covered every surface in the shop. Mother was glad to have a job, hard as it was. Father's salary would not have been enough to cover our needs. When she developed lung problems later in

Audra's 2nd grade school picture.

life, I suspect her disease may be traced back to the fiber dust she breathed for about ten years in that factory.

Our Vinton Street house was not far from Dorchester Bay, so on weekends our parents took us walking along the beach. We walked for miles. On one of those walks, father spotted an area that he liked, a nicer neighborhood — Savin Hill in Dorchester. Once he found another dilapidated house that he could afford to buy, we moved again.

Chapter X: Savin Hill

If asked, where are you from, where did you grow up? I answer today: Boston. But I think immediately: my Savin Hill home. I think all my siblings would answer the same way. When we moved there in the spring of 1954, I was ten, Rimas eight, Algis and Dana six.

I fell in love with the house the minute I saw it — a graceful Victorian with a veranda all around. It had a wide front lawn, a separate garage, and space for a large vegetable garden on one side. Behind the property grew a narrow strip of woods. Beyond that, the blue waters of Dorchester Bay stretched out into the distance. If we cut through a neighbor's property, we could be at a sandy swimming beach in five minutes. There was a tree-covered hill in the middle of the neighborhood, with tennis and basketball courts at the bottom and steep rock cliffs higher up. In summer, we risked our lives clambering up those cliffs, without the benefit of

Dana, Kazys and Audra stand in front of the already renovated house in Savin Hill. It was the showpiece of the neighborhood and a wonderful place to grow up.

rock climbing equipment. In winter, the hill was a sledding paradise. What a wonderful place for children to grow up! We were out of the slums! Now we walked to the Savin Hill station along a tree-lined street and took the subway train to South Boston, to St. Peter's school, still by ourselves. We had moved up in the world!

The house itself was indeed dilapidated — father had a many-year project ahead of him to make it livable. It was not an easy task, as he recalled. *A real estate agent showed us a house at 235 Savin Hill Avenue that was for sale in a lovely location: on a spacious lot near the seashore. From two sides of the house* we could see the bays. The house was large — two and a half floors — with four bedrooms, but very old (perhaps more than a hundred years old) and badly neglected. For that reason the price was low. That's just the kind of house we needed. We scarcely had any savings but lots of energy, since we were young and experienced from renovating the old house on Vinton Street. Without any delay, we moved here in the spring of 1954. Just at that time my company had fewer projects, so in January 1955 I was let go. I was out of work for about five months but received unemployment benefits. I used all that time for renovation. Once I started working again, I continued the renovation projects after work and on weekends. It took us about two years to get the house more or less in order. All that sweat and dust took its toll on my health. My TB flared up and a doctor wanted to send me off to a sanatorium. I argued against that, saying: who will take care of my family? A commission of two doctors examined me and the second one finally agreed to let me be treated at home. That second doctor concluded that I was an intelligent person with good hygiene, thus unlikely to infect other people. The treatment for TB was free of charge — I received a large bottle full of pills that I had to swallow daily in huge quantities. Periodically I went in for x-rays. I don't remember exactly how long this treatment lasted, probably not less than a year, until I was considered fully cured.

I found temporary employment with Fay Spoffort & Thorndike Co. as an electrical designer for the Boston Expressway tunnel for which I planned the energy requirements and lighting installations. I worked there for three months, from May through July of 1955, until the project was completed. While working there, I got along very well with my boss, so when the project ended, he said, "Kazys, don't worry. I will find you another job." And that's what happened. He gave me a very good recommendation and sent me to a large company, Chas. T. Main. Before I went there, he called my future boss to make sure he hired me. I started to work for this company in July 1955 as an electrical designer and continued there without a break for 22 years, until I retired on February 27, 1977. I mostly worked on designing large hydroelectric power plants. Our company designed and supervised the construction of mega-projects such as the St. Lawrence Power Plant, the Niagara Power Plant, the Blenheim-Gilboa Project and many others. My superiors respected me and trusted my abilities as a good professional. There were periods when the company did not have enough projects and had to dismiss some employees but they never dismissed me.

Our life in Savin Hill was convenient: the area was beautiful and the subway station close by. In a few minutes we could get to work and the children could attend the Catholic school at St. Peter's parish in South Boston. They also went there on Saturdays to a Lithuanian language school. Close by were sports fields and a tree-covered hill where the boys could let out their energy. We also *had a beach close by that was still clean in those days. I worked the soil to create a wonderful garden — we had enough vegetables from early spring to late fall. We even had enough to share with friends and neighbors. I planted a large number of raspberry bushes, so many that the children grew tired of picking and eating the berries. We even had our own grapes from which I made good wine in the fall. I kept several beehives and used the leftover honey to make mead. For Easter one spring we bought*

Audra, in white, in the Saturday Lithuanian language school — šeštadieninė.

Dana, sitting in the front on the right, and Algis, at the back of that row, also finished 12 years of "Saturday School."

about twenty baby chicks, so the children could enjoy them. They grew rapidly and began to lay eggs. Every day we had our own fresh eggs that we ate with pleasure — much more delicious than the store-bought variety. No one worried about cholesterol at that time. We enjoyed these eggs for about three years, until the chickens got old and we had to liquidate them.

When we first moved to Boston, Jadzė had found work in a sewing factory in South Boston. She reached the factory by bus. Only in 1956 did we purchase our first car, a used Oldsmobile. While we had no car, I found time to travel by bus to City Point in South Boston where I fished. I caught flounders and eels; the latter were delicious when smoked. Often I took the boys along, if they were interested. As soon as we bought the car, there was no more time for fishing because then we wanted to drive further, to see other interesting places.

All in all, Savin Hill was a good place to raise our children. We adults also

Kazys (fourth from right) acting in a play put on by the Boston Drama Group.

enjoyed living there. We were still young and had many good, lively friends. These friends often gathered at our house because we had a large living room where we could dance, sing and party. When I look back, I can't comprehend how we found the time for all the things we did. Besides work, we had an active social and cultural life. Jadzė and I both belonged to the Boston chapter of the Ateitininkai organization. I was a member of the Boston Lithuanian Engineers Association. Jadzė sang in two choirs: the church choir led by composer Jeronimas Kačinskas and a choir led by composer Julius Gaidelis. From the beginning I was involved in the Boston Drama Group where I played the leading roles for a number of years. Our directors were at first Aleksandra Gustaitienė, followed by Henrikas Kačinskas, one of the foremost actors in pre-war Lithuania. Later, I also joined the Boston Modern Theater Group whose director was Beatričė Kerbelienė. We rehearsed several times a week.

I see myself walking along Savin Hill Avenue, our house with the red tile roof, the white clapboard siding and green ornaments coming into view. Crossing the lawn I climb up to the veranda that encircled the entire house when we first moved in. What fun it was to race around and around, entering the house through windows that reached down to the floor. This fun lasted only a short time. Much to our sorrow, father decided it would cost too much time and money to replace the rotten wood, so he pulled down the veranda on two sides of the house, leaving only the front and back. He even raised the windows for the sake of heating economy. Stepping through the front door, I enter the hallway and look around. The staircase to the second floor is straight ahead of me. But to the left, through the sliding door, is the enormous living room that takes up the entire half of the first floor. When father pulled out the sliding door to fix it, he felt something soft at the far end. It was a hand-sewn American flag with thirteen stars and stripes. How old was it? Did it really date back to the American Revolution? Why did someone hide it at the back of a sliding door? We never found out the answers to these questions. We made an effort at one time to find a home for the flag in a museum, but no one wanted it. There were too many old flags in the Boston area. I don't know what became of the flag after that.

The old 13-star American flag had plenty of moth-holes. We were so disappointed that no one wanted this old relic.

At the far end of the living room is a seating arrangement — a sofa, coffee table and some soft chairs. The ceiling is high and the long drapes mother made match the light grey color of the wallpaper and carpet. Mother had wallpapered the living room mostly by herself, with some help from us children. Here, at the entrance to the room, the wooden floor is bare. A piano and a record player stand between the windows. Mother had spent hour after hour on her knees, installing the oak floorboards. We children pitched in after school. Dana remembers drilling the holes in the hard oak boards, then hammering in the nails. Our knees were killing us, but we made progress; eventually the immense room was finished. We sanded the floor, creating clouds of dust; finally, we brushed on several layers of varnish. Mother kept the beautiful wooden floor nicely polished, ready for a party, for dancing. From the hallway to the right is our father's study, the room where he sat at his desk drawing plans, paying bills, writing letters, and filling three small notebooks of his memoirs with his clear, precise writing. If we heard him declaiming to himself, we knew he was practicing his role for the next theater performance. Further up the hall and to the right is the large kitchen with a window toward the back yard and another toward the side, with a view of lilac bushes blooming in the spring. Returning from work, out of breath, with two large grocery bags in each arm, mother worked fast to put our evening meal on the table. Dana and I hung

Official family portrait taken in 1960, 11 years after our arrival in the United States.

out with her, chopping the onions or running out to the garden to pick the lettuce. Mother was in a rush but almost always cheerful, singing along as she cooked. Her singing was so constant, that one day when she wasn't singing, Dana found it strange and asked her why she had stopped. She said, "Oh, I didn't think you noticed."

While the boys watched TV upstairs, mother beckoned Dana and me into the pantry to show us what she had brought home from the store. "Quick, girls," she said. "Eat some of this, before the boys find it." Rimas and Algis, growing fast and always hungry, devoured everything they could get their hands on. A half-gallon of ice cream disappeared in one sitting; a bag of oranges turned instantly into a pile of peels and seeds. The pantry where mother hid the goodies was a special place. It had a dumb waiter that connected the kitchen to the basement. The original kitchen for the house had been in the basement and from there, in the old days, the cook would send up the prepared food to the main floor for dining. Next to the kitchen was a small room with a stained glass window toward the back yard. Here, at a large, round oak table we spent some of our happiest hours. Meals were always family affairs. The parents wanted to hear how we had spent the day. Father attempted to recruit us for his endless projects, not usually with much success. "I have homework," was always an effective excuse, because for him, school and learning had priority above all else; he expected us to do well in school. On Christmas Eve, mother covered the round table with her best white linen tablecloth for here we ate our special meal, kūčios. As teenagers we gathered at that round table with our friends and dates, sitting there until the wee hours of the morning, joking, laughing — our parents fast asleep upstairs.

In my mind I walk up the stairs, remembering where the floorboards squeak. I step over those spots cautiously to avoid waking the parents; they mustn't know how late it is. To the left of the upstairs landing is our bathroom with the deep claw-foot tub. How many times did I pound on the door to get someone out of there faster? Otherwise, I'd have to run all the way down to the basement where we had another toilet and a small shower. Straight ahead — our parents' bedroom. Further along is the library — a room paneled in dark wood and featuring a built-in sofa with an armrest in the shape of a lion's head. All around are shelves for books, but our TV also stands here. There had been a fireplace here once, but it was in such bad repair that father blocked it off, as he did with all the other fireplaces in the house. This is a beautiful room, I think, like a room in an old English manor. Mother read us our bedtime stories here, on that couch — fairy tales in Lithuanian, or the poem "Meškiukas Rudnosiukas," (Little Brown-Nosed Bear) a favorite of ours. Next to the library is the tiny room that belongs to Dana. At first she and I had slept together in one room, in one bed, until father finished his renovations. Now we each have our own. At the far end of the hallway I approach my room. Across from me is the boys' room, noisy and disorderly. How they fought in there, wrestling and rolling over each other — was it in play or in earnest? It was hard to tell. They fought so hard that one of them poked his foot into the wall by the bed and made a big hole in the plaster. Father was not pleased.

Compared to that room of male strife and competition, mine was an oasis of peace. There was a niche in the wall with a sink — a feature I greatly appreciated. When I sat on the sill of my open window, I looked down at the street, the trees, and in the distance the blue water of the bay. With the door closed, ignoring the shouts from the boys' room, I could sit and dream for hours. I dreamt of far away places, of adventures I had read about. Always on the side of the Indians in the novels of the West by Zane Grey, I copied out words in the native languages and planned to learn how to speak "Indian." Some day I would go far away from here, see the world, have marvelous adventures. Dana often begged me to tell her stories. I entertained her for hours with the yarns I spun.

On the attic floor above were four mysterious rooms. One was finished,

Visiting father's cousin and her husband in Buffalo, NY.

the other three lacked floorboards or wall paneling. We liked to hide out up there, making up games and finding odd things. In one of the rooms, father decided to raise exotic pigeons — one of his crazier ideas. He obtained from somewhere two beautiful pigeons, one male and one female; soon they had laid eggs and

hatched some baby birds. Father opened the window, thinking that the adults would return with food for the babies. First, the male bird flew away, so he closed the window. Once the eggs hatched, he opened it again, thinking the mother would not desert the babies — but he was wrong. He was left with a nest of baby birds in his attic room. What to do? It was too painful to let them starve. After some research, he brought them dried split peas. But the baby birds could not pick up the split peas with their beaks. Someone had to chew the peas until they were mushy, then place each little bird's head in one's mouth, so it could feed in the way it had been fed by the parents who had abandoned them. Father recruited Dana and me for this project; we felt sorry for the birds and fed them for a while. I disliked going into that room. When I opened the doors, the frightened baby birds flapped around. The floor was covered with bird poop and split peas lay scattered everywhere. What a mess! Mother continued to feed the birds after Dana gave up and I was "too busy with homework." The boys refused to take part in this project. After all our trouble, when the pigeons were full-grown, father killed them and persuaded mother to cook them. He was the only one who would eat them; he admitted they were very tough.

In the walkout basement was another set of rooms: there was a huge coal furnace that father later converted to oil heat; a storage bin for potatoes; the area where our chickens lived, while we had them; father's work and tool room;

the former kitchen; even a shower and toilet were there, used by father when he came in from the garden. Father had created a mini-farm in the middle of the city, with birds and bees, vegetables and berries. He was and always remained a farmer at heart — he loved the soil. Long before most people thought about it, he was against chemical sprays and artificial fertilizers. Once a month, the magazine "Organic Gardening" arrived in the mail and he eagerly perused it for suggestions: how to keep the weeds down, how to get rid of bugs without pesticides. He decided once that our front lawn needed fertilizing. Instead of spreading chemical fertilizers like his neighbors, he had a truckload of manure delivered and proceeded to spread it all over the lawn. For weeks, people could smell our

Our first automobile, a '49 Oldsmobile 88. Mother said the reverse gear didn't work.

house before they could see it. I found it embarrassing and refused to bring friends home while it lasted.

After school we were on our own until mother returned from work. Summer days were also ours to spend as we wished, except for Sundays, when we all went to Mass and frequently took excursions to a park or to Cape Cod. We loved strolling in the Arnold Arboretum in Boston, admiring the exotic plants from around the world. Father studied their labels, while the boys raced ahead to play hide-and-go-seek. We took a few memorable family car trips. One was to Niagara Falls, where we got a private tour of the power plant after father introduced himself as the electrical designer who had signed off on the plans. The staff immediately recognized his name, so father walked around proudly, like a proprietor. We traveled to Pennsylvania to visit father's relatives who had settled in the mining town of Shenandoah in the early part of the 20th century. We visited his cousin near the city of Hamilton in Canada. Driving along in our black Oldsmobile, we four sat in the back with our legs up on the front seats or stuck out the side windows. These were the days before seat belts. Mother usually drove and sang for us, one song after the other, while father watched over the map. We were quite a circus!

The twins' graduation from 8th grade — Audra was an usher.

We had few toys but no lack of imagination, making up games that lasted all day. Down in the woods below our house I had a special tree that I climbed for daydreaming, where Dana and Algis could join me when they wanted to hear stories. We had a "sacred" rock buried in a special place and all sorts of weird rituals. Dana liked to play house; I kept at it to keep her company, long after I lost interest in dolls. We made her our princess and dressed her up in special attire. When we were older, mother taught Dana and me to sew, crochet and embroider. We happily made clothes that we could not afford to buy. The younger children in the neighborhood adored Algis. They came around asking: is Al home? Can he come out to play? With great patience, Algis, by then in his teens, tossed the ball with them and spent hours at the basketball court teaching them to play. Tall, strong, and a natural athlete, he played on the Boston Lithuanian basketball team, a team known for its aggressive prowess.

We became independent early, but the flip side was that we did not have much supervision. Our parents set down the rules and expected us to obey. They often did not know the mischief we got into, until it was too late. This was the negative side of our parents' struggle to succeed in this new country: it left them with little time for the children. And they did not understand the dangers and temptations that surrounded us. They parented us as though they were still living in a small town or village in Lithuania, where the community kept its collective eye on the children. Rimas was a special problem: from early on he was an alienated, angry, unhappy boy. As a middle child, he may have felt stuck between his slightly older, "smart" sister, who was father's favorite, and the twins who, being the youngest, got the most attention. And besides, the twins were cute — everyone admired them. Dana and mother were especially close and Algis was a good-natured boy who did not protest when father recruited him to help, in place of the ever-absent Rimas. Algis went along with tasks he found distasteful, as when father decided it was time to "liquidate" the chickens and Al had to help chop off their heads — a traumatic experience for a sensitive boy. He worked with father one hot summer to repaint our entire house, going up and down high ladders — a dangerous undertaking.

Rimas, in the meantime, hung out with friends who got him into trouble — fights, alcohol and the like. He stopped studying, began to skip school, drank alcohol from the parents' cabinet and took money from mother's wallet. For our parents, for whom honesty was an absolute value, this was shocking. Mother tried to reason kindly with Rimas but could not manage him. Father disciplined him in the traditional way, by spanking. The entire family was exhausted and terrified after those awful spanking scenes. When Rimas dropped out of one high school or was suspended, the parents put him in another. To get him away from his pals, they sent him to the Franciscan Lithuanian boarding school in Kennebunkport, Maine, for a year, hoping the monks would instill in him some discipline and desire for learning. When he came home unreformed, they put him in a trade school so he might learn a practical skill that could carry him through life. In spite of all their efforts and pleadings, Rimas dropped out of school before earning a high school diploma. He enrolled in the Marine

Dana made a drawing of the house in Savin Hill, which she loved very much. It now hangs in my bedroom.

Corps; again, our parents hoped this might put him on a straighter path. However, during basic training, it was discovered that he had a kidney problem resulting from a childhood illness. The Marine Corps gave him a medical discharge. Rimas was highly intelligent. When later in life he wanted a high school equivalency degree, he took the GED (General Education Diploma) and passed the exam in one shot. He read a lot and he spoke and wrote well. From early on, and for about twenty years, he was dependent on alcohol.

All of our parents' social life and much of ours was based in the Lithuanian community. We went to community picnics, concerts, theater performances, and on Sundays to the Lithuanian Catholic Mass at St. Peter's Church. The folk dance group taught by Mrs. Ivaškienė in South Boston was great fun. We even traveled to other cities to perform. The various youth organizations had dances and

The Boston folk dance group (Samburis) was invited to dance in Washington DC and to a reception at the Lithuanian Embassy. Audra is second girl from the left and Dana is the first girl from the right.

parties; we sang Lithuanian folk songs, enjoyed the traditions, the special foods. It was a close-knit society that offered a sense of belonging — Lithuanian young people "clicked" with one another wherever they met. But best of all were the two weeks at summer camp, to which Lithuanian youth came from around the country. Our parents sent us to a camp for two weeks every summer that was run by the Lithuanian organization "Ateitininkai." Sometimes the camp was held in Manomet, Massachusetts, sometimes in Kennebunkport, Maine. One year we were thrilled when mother went with us to camp to serve as a volunteer counselor. At age sixteen I was permitted to travel to Michigan by bus, to a large camp called "Dainava," where Lithuanian young people from Chicago gathered — an interesting group of new friends. The camp atmosphere was joyful; we were active and happy all day and then sang around the bonfire at night. Here we made friends who remained our friends for life.

Our parents, the organizations, the Saturday school classes all taught us the same lesson: to love our lost country Lithuania. We were raised to be patriotic, to hate the Communist system that brought so much suffering to our country, to hope for a day when Lithuania would be free once again. We learned to take pride in Lithuania's grand medieval history, its ancient language, beautiful poetry, literature, and folk art. The picture of Lithuania presented to us was idealized and romanticized. It seemed like a mythical place. We empathized with our parents' nostalgia for the land they had lost, their longing for the relatives left behind. We observed how eagerly our parents read the first letters that reached them from relatives in Lithuania, how they yearned for news from home. Until they read those first letters, they did not know which relatives were alive, who had perished, who might have been deported to Siberia. After contact started, mother spent countless hours and a good portion of her earnings buying items and packaging them for mailing to the relatives. She constantly had a package in the works, alternating between father's relatives and her own. Since they had many siblings, there was always someone who needed help. Our parents lived frugally but were generous to others when they saw hardship.

Our Lithuanian community life in Boston gave us many benefits: we were bilingual, we belonged to a close-knit group, and we acquired values that made us feel distinct from other Americans. However, this kind of life tended to limit the way we interacted with American culture. As I grew older, I

Opening Christmas presents in the enormous living room in Savin Hill, 1963.

became impatient with what I began to feel was a psychological ghetto. I wanted to break out, to step into a wider playing field, to see America and the world for myself.

I began to walk the road from Savin Hill station to my lovely Victorian home when I was ten years old, with long braids swinging down my back. One day, on that walk, I realized with surprise, that my inner language had changed from Lithuanian to English. That was a milestone for me. Later, I trudged on that same path, in my ugly uniform, from Cardinal Cushing Central High School for Girls, a Catholic school that our parents selected, not because of the academics (which were poor) but because they expected the nuns to teach us proper values. Dana followed in my footsteps to the same high school and disliked it as much as I did.

I continued the same walk home for four more years while I commuted to Emmanuel College in Boston, again a Catholic school for girls, run by the same nuns: the Sisters of Notre Dame de Namur. The college had offered me a tuition scholarship and living at home was free — financially a good deal. I knew my parents were just scraping by, so I was eager to support myself. I had started to earn my own pocket money with babysitting jobs as a teenager. One summer I spent a memorable two weeks living with the noted archeologist, Dr. Maria Gimbutas, taking care of her youngest daughter Rasa. Once I turned sixteen and could work officially, I spent the summers working in a shoe factory, a hospital, and as a filing clerk in an office. With these summer savings I paid for my college texts. At Emmanuel College I decided to major in German and minor in Spanish, with the dream that I would become a foreign correspondent for an American newspaper and travel the world. After two years of classroom German, I realized I needed to live in that country, if I hoped to gain any fluency. I enrolled in an inexpensive work/travel program and went off to spend the summer in Germany where I worked in a family-operated hotel near the Black Forest. My parents let me go without objections, especially since I had my own savings to pay for the travel. They allowed me to plan my own life and I did not ask them for advice, believing their experience in America was too limited.

Dana and Audra at Savin Hill beach in 1964.

The return trip to Germany was exciting! I was eager to see again the country that I vaguely remembered from my childhood.

In order to improve my Spanish fluency, I signed up for a summer of volunteer work in Peru and traveled there in 1964 with about a dozen other girls from Emmanuel College. They all stayed in Lima while I went on alone by bus to the south of the country, to Arequipa. I lived with a middle class family and worked with the native Quechua people who lived in great poverty, in slums around the city. Every morning, I accompanied a Catholic nun, sitting behind her on her scooter, her white robe flying in my face, as we visited family compounds to check on sick women. This trip opened my eyes — I saw how people lived in the third world, the unimaginable poverty and misery. The daughter of my host family and I traveled to the famous Inca cities of Cusco and Machu Picchu — a fabulous sight that my husband Klaus and I returned to again in 2012. We managed to reconnect with my host family from the summer of 1964 and to visit them once more in Arequipa. These first trips abroad, while still in college, whetted my appetite for more. By the time I graduated from Emmanuel College in 1965, age 22, I was more than ready to turn my back on Savin Hill and all it stood for in my life. I yearned to reach out to a larger world.

Chapter XI: The Birds Leave the Nest

By 1965 the Barūnas children began to scatter in different directions. When I graduated from Emmanuel College in spring 1965, I was the first to leave home. With the support of a Fulbright Fellowship I studied for a year at the University of Mainz, Germany. After that, I entered the Ph.D. program in German literature at Stanford University in California, my studies financed by a Woodrow Wilson fellowship. There, in my first semester, in the fall of 1966, I met and fell in love with Klaus Willeke. The following summer Dana came to live with me in Palo Alto during her college vacation. She met Klaus, my Stanford friends, and came to love California as I did.

Next to leave home was Rimvydas who married Janice Mahan in1967. Although Algis and Dana were still living with the parents, commuting to their colleges, our parents realized that the last two children would soon be leaving as well. Father wrote:

We lived in the Savin Hill house until 1968, for almost fifteen years. In that time, the children grew up, finished their studies and began to disperse into the wide world. While we were still living in Savin Hill, Rimvydas got married in 1967 [September 16] to Janice Mahan. The Rimvydas got married in 1967 while we lived in Savin Hill. Some of our yard is visible.

following year, on November 1, 1968, their daughter Kristina was born [in Cambridge, Massachusetts]. But by 1969, Rimvydas had left his family and begun a wandering gypsy life. Audronė married Klaus Willeke on June 29, 1968. Only Algis and Danutė remained with us and they were in the last year of college. As our family shrank, the house became too large. Besides, it was old and outdated. I began to think about building a new, smaller house somewhere in the suburbs. I found a plot in the town of Hingham, about twenty miles south of Boston, on a new street, Hazelwood Drive, just off Route 53. It was an attractive lot, covered

Audra's wedding in 1968, with Rimas on one arm and bridegroom Klaus on the other.

with young pines and oak trees. I sketched out the plans and started to build the house in spring 1968. I didn't use a contractor — I bought the building materials myself and hired people for specific jobs.

1968 was a complicated year, since not only was I building the house, but we were also preparing a lovely wedding for Audronė that summer. We moved into the new house before Christmas that same year and were delighted. As usual, I threw myself with full vigor into making the environment as attractive as possible. Roses and other flowers were soon blooming around the house; I planted grapes, raspberries, and a vegetable garden. Our old friends visited us often and our life was happy here. The one thing I missed was the ocean. For so many years we had lived within view of the bay, while from here the ocean was rather far and the closest beach not suitable for swimming. As my retirement approached, I started to think: what will I do here once I'm retired? All the work around the house was finished and it's not in my nature to do nothing.

Father does not mention that mother's health was adversely affected by the stress of job and home. In 1970, around Christmas, she landed in the hospital with what appeared to be a heart attack but in fact was later diagnosed to be a nervous condition. Dana returned from Germany and stayed for three months to care for her. When she returned to Munich she had to start all over again, looking for work and a place to live. Mother continued to have such heart palpitations regularly.

While father and mother were settling into their Hingham house and perfecting the garden, Klaus and I, newly married, prepared to leave Stanford University for a year in Germany. Klaus received his Ph.D. in Aeronautics/Astronautics in the spring of 1969, marching down the aisle of the

Stanford stadium to pick up his diploma with a psychedelic, pink and blue tie that I had made for him hanging over his black robe. We had witnessed the "summer of love," participated in the protest marches against the war in Vietnam, hiked and camped in the Sierras, and had fallen in love with California. But in spring 1969 we had our careers to pursue. I still needed to write my dissertation on the German expressionist author Frank Wedekind, whose archive was in Munich. The German government granted me a DAAD fellowship for this research; Klaus found a postdoctoral position at the Max Planck Institute in Garching, a suburb of Munich. So off we went, not knowing if we would ever return to our beloved San Francisco Bay area.

Klaus had immigrated to the United States with his family at age nineteen with a diploma from a German "Gymnasium" (secondary school), so he was perfectly fluent in both English and German. He also spoke French well and was as avid a traveler as I was. Before settling down to work in Munich, we spent the summer of 1969 traveling by car through Eastern Europe: from Austria we drove through Yugoslavia to Greece, Turkey, Bulgaria, Rumania (where Klaus presented a paper at a conference), Hungary, and Poland. Traveling through the Soviet republics, behind the "Iron Curtain," brought us some amazing experiences, some unexpected challenges. That trip is a story in itself.

Arriving in Warsaw, we parked our car and took the train to Vilnius, Lithuania, for a five-day visit. This was the first time that a member of our American family had returned to Lithuania since our parents fled in 1944. We had sent a postcard to say we were coming and about fifty relatives lined the train platform in Vilnius, with flowers in their hands, to greet us. It was an emotional reunion. Here were the uncles, aunts, and cousins I had seen in photos. They had taken time off from work, traveled from all parts of Lithuania to meet and talk with us. There were so many of them — we wanted to spend some time with each one. Those days in Vilnius were overwhelming and intense. While I talked, held hands, and hugged my relatives, Klaus went walking around the drab and neglected city with KGB agents following him at a visible distance. There were not many Western tourists in Vilnius that September, so we had lots of "protection" wherever we went. Soviet rules did not permit us to leave the city, but some of my relatives wanted us to travel to the countryside, to visit the cemeteries where my ancestors were buried. They had prepared a feast and wanted to host us in good Lithuanian tradition in their homes.

My cousin Edvardas Bolisas, a successful construction engineer and member of the communist party, owned a car; he thought he could smuggle us out of Vilnius. But there was surely eavesdropping equipment installed in our hotel room, so the authorities got wind of the plan. Just as we drove beyond the city limits, a white Volga car passed us and blocked the road. Russian soldiers

On their first visit to Vilnius in 1969, Audra and Klaus were greeted at the train station by about 50 relatives, flowers in hand.

with rifles jumped out, threw out the relatives riding in the car, got in and ordered our driver, cousin Edvardas, to turn around and drive back to Vilnius. This was scary stuff — but this was our last day in Lithuania and next morning we departed by train, as scheduled. Nothing happened to us, but we worried about our brave cousin Edvardas, especially since we did not hear from him for a long time. Years later, we learned he had been interrogated by the KGB about the incident. Since he had well-placed friends in the Party, the KGB merely gave him a warning and nothing more.

After the emotion-filled days in Vilnius, Klaus and I returned to Warsaw to pick up our car, and via Czechoslovakia, drove back to Germany to start our work in Munich. For me it was important to have seen Lithuania, if only briefly, the country I had heard so much about. I returned to Lithuania for a longer visit in the summer of 1973, when I participated in a six-week course at the University of Vilnius. There was a bit of a "thaw" in the relations with the West by then so I was able to travel to Kaunas, stay in cousin Edvardas Bolisas' apartment and get to know him and his family better. Our contacts with Lithuania, in both directions, intensified after the country regained independence in 1990. I'll talk about that in a later chapter.

In the meantime, back in Hingham, Dana had graduated from the Massachusetts College of Art in spring1969 and, following my invitation, came to stay with Klaus and me in Munich, after our return from Lithuania. My idea was that before starting to work, she would enjoy seeing a bit of Europe. I first booked her on a young people's bus trip to Spain. When Dana arrived in Munich, she knew no German, so I enrolled her in an eight-week intensive language course at the University of Munich and by the end of the course she was able to converse in a rudimentary way. Klaus and I had expected her to stay with us for a few months. However, she fell in love with Munich and wanted to stay longer, so she looked for, and found, a job. When Klaus and I left in spring 1970 to work at the University of Minnesota, she stayed on in Germany for the next thirteen years where she made a good life for herself. She worked in advertising, traveled all over Europe, and made good friends. When mother had what was thought to be a heart attack around Christmas 1971, Dana returned to take care of her for three months, but felt she needed to go back to Munich. There she had to start all over again looking for a job and an apartment. Algis came to visit in 1972 and together they toured Europe. She invited the parents to come in 1978 — their first trip to Europe since leaving the camps in 1949. They were amazed at the transformation of West Germany. With Dana they traveled to Italy, all the way down to Rome. Dana still considers her time in Munich as the best years of her life.

She also visited Lithuania a couple of times while living in Munich and was overwhelmed at setting foot on Lithuanian soil. Growing up she had thought of our "homeland" as a fairytale-land which we would probably never see.

In 1980 Dana began to consider moving back to the United States. Returning for a visit to the States that summer, she took the parents on a trip to California, wanting to see if she would like to live in the US again.

Dana, center, surrounded by cousins on her first visit to Lithuania..

Her verdict was negative, but still she continued with her plans to move back. In October 1981, she was seriously injured in a near-fatal car accident on a drive from Munich to Bonn. Mother and I flew to see her in the Bonn hospital and stayed a week, until we were convinced she was out of danger and getting good care. After three months she was sent home to Munich, where she still had to undergo extensive rehab. In September of 1982 she moved back to the Boston area to be near the parents who were then living in Manomet. But she had become a "European" and immediately regretted her move.

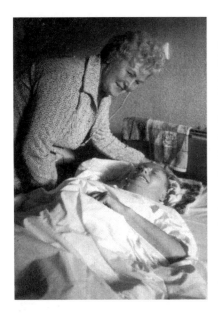

Mother at Dana's hospital bed, in Bonn, 1981, after the horrific car accident.

Algis also graduated in 1969, with a degree in Business Administration from Boston College. Not happy with the prospect of sitting behind a desk all day, he went back to school to earn a teaching certificate. For several years, he taught math and other subjects in a middle school north of Boston. He was a gifted and creative teacher, much loved and respected by the students. After three years, he received tenure in his position. The administration, however, did not support his innovative teaching methods. So, disappointed and frustrated, he quit teaching. After he married Virginia (Ginny) Hoffman on April 24, 1975, he moved with her to St. Paul, Minnesota where he earned a Bachelor's degree in Irrigational Engineering at the University of Minnesota. This was a wonderful turn of events, because Klaus and I were still working at the University. When we left in 1976 for greener pastures in Ohio, Algis and Ginny remained in Minnesota for one more year. Algis inherited from Klaus a huge, blue down jacket with a hood that kept him warm in the bitter-cold Minnesota winters. They, too, were glad to leave Minnesota behind, moving to New Jersey, where Algis found a job in his new field of irrigational engineering. Their next move took them to New Hampshire, to the Laconia area, where Algis, once again, changed his career path. He started a successful house painting business with several employees. Their daughter, Laura, was born in New Hampshire on April 20, 1981, and their son, Alex, on January 16, 1985. Now our parents had four grandchildren, Kristina, Thomas (Vytas), Laura, and Alex — all very precious to them. The grandchildren referred to their grandparents by the Lithuanian words Močiutė (grandmother) and Tėvukas (grandfather).

Algis and Ginny cut their wedding cake.

When Klaus accepted a faculty position in the Department of Mechanical Engineering at the University of Minnesota, he shifted his research to a new field — from aeronautics/ astronautics to aerosol science. After we arrived in Minnesota, I continued work on my dissertation and received the Ph.D. degree in German literature from Stanford University in 1974. At the University of Minnesota I taught in temporary positions in the German Department and the Humanities Program. In 1975, I switched to a job in University administration. Our son Thomas (name later changed to Vytas) was born on May 7, 1974. Klaus and I had to learn to be parents without the support of our families who were all living far away. We enjoyed our small, cottage-like house dwarfed by giant elm trees in the neighbor-

Thomas Klaus Willeke was born in Minnesota in 1974.

hood of St. Anthony Park, St. Paul. In spite of the cold winters, Minnesota had much to offer. We strolled around the city lakes in summer and enjoyed cross-country skiing in winter. Before Thomas (Vytas) was born, we canoed in the lake country bordering on Canada for two weeks, together with our friends Janina and Gintaras Rėklaitis and Algis, who joined us from Boston. This wilderness experience remains a unique memory.

In 1976, we left Minnesota when we found better career opportunities for both of us in Cincinnati, Ohio. Klaus accepted a faculty position in the Department of Environmental Health at the University of Cincinnati; I taught German at nearby Miami University of Ohio. We bought a house in the Cincinnati suburb of Wyoming, at 147 Ritchie Avenue, where Thomas (Vytas) grew up. Klaus and I traveled extensively for professional reasons and also because we enjoyed it, taking Thomas with us on many of the trips. We spent extended periods of time in Japan and in Europe, primarily in Germany. During our most adventurous sabbatical year, 1983–84, we spent six months in Europe on our research projects. Then we continued around the world, lecturing in Egypt, Thailand, Singapore, Indonesia, China, and Japan. Thomas celebrated his tenth birthday with an Egyptian family in Cairo. In his teen years, Thomas belonged to an organization called Society for Creative Anachronism (SCA), a role-playing group that reenacted the Middle Ages. He took the name Vytas, in honor of the Lithuanian Grand Duke Vytautas, and this gradually became the name he was known by. In 2005, at the time of his marriage, he changed his legal name from Thomas to Vytas, so from this point on I will refer to him as Vytas. Vytas graduated from the Seven Hills High School in 1992 and was accepted at Stanford University but delayed his studies for a year in order to join Klaus and me for another sabbatical year in Munich. All three of us visited Lithuania that year; it was Vytas' second visit and the highlight for him this time was mushroom picking in the forests. With a U-rail pass and Youth Hostel card he traveled on his own throughout Europe and in the Middle East, an important rite of passage to adulthood.

About a year after their wedding, Rimas left his wife Janice and baby daughter Kristina. He lived for a while in Canada, taking refuge with our father's cousin near Calgary. Later, he migrated further to Utah, then down to Texas. He did hard physical labor: in construction, in lumber camps, in the oil fields, all the time pursued by the twin demons alcohol and drugs. We got periodic news about him, or calls from him, when he was desperate for money. Dana remembers that Rimas would call her periodically in Munich, the only family member to do so. He was usually intoxicated and missing his family. Our parents were never sure where he was or whether he was still alive. They were dismayed by his life style and by the fact that he had deserted his wife and child. Our parents loved their first grandchild and tried to have as much contact with her as possible. Mother would frequently pick up Kristina on weekends and was glad that Janice agreed to this. They developed a close relationship.

When the parents built their house in Hingham, mother was working for the Gillette company, located in South Boston. She had found a job there in 1966, delighted to leave the dust and noise of the clothing factory behind her. At Gillette she received a better salary and benefits, and the working conditions were pleasant. She was proud and pleased when after a

Mother with Thomas and Kristina in Plymouth, summer of '79.

few years she was promoted to quality inspector. Mother did not complain about the additional twenty-mile drive from Hingham to South Boston. But the situation changed radically when father found, and purchased, a building site in Manomet, near Plymouth, sixty miles south of Boston. Father, motivated by his desire to live by the sea and always eager for a new project, paid scant attention to mother's situation. He did not consult with her before he bought that property. The results of his self-centered action were dire and could have cost both of them their lives. It is interesting to note that he does not mention this in his memoir.

I started to look for a place by the ocean. I found such a place in the historic town of Plymouth, or rather in Manomet, a suburb of Plymouth. From the small hill one had a perfect view of the ocean and in front there was a large meadow. The area was sparsely inhabited, somewhat wild. Delighted by the view of the ocean, with no delay, I bought this lot. I have to say that it is almost impossible to find a building site near the ocean or the price is usually prohibitive. I made this purchase at the start of 1974. When I started to build the house, I still had three years to go until retirement. Some of the construction I did myself, for some of it I hired people. I used up all my weekends for this work and my vacation days, which I took one

Kazys standing in his garden at the house in Manomet with the ocean view in back.

day each week. When I retired, I worked on the house non-stop and apparently overdid it. I suffered my first heart attack and ended up in intensive care for two weeks. We sold the Hingham house and moved into the new one in the summer of 1977. We thought this would be our final move.

While father, now retired, was enjoying the ocean views and his new garden projects, mother continued to commute to work at the Gillette Company, sixty miles each way. Her shift started in the afternoon and her drive home was late at night — she returned around midnight. Some nights she became sleepy and needed to stop half way, in a highway rest stop, to take a short nap. In the winters, she often faced hazardous road conditions. It took a lot of concentration to drive through ice and snow at night. Before she reached home, she regularly stopped at a 24-hour grocery store to stock up on food. Eventually, she found a room with a Lithuanian family in South Boston, where, in winter, she would stay all week, returning home on the

The last photo of our whole family together on the twins' 40th birthday, 1987. We're holding our "little birds."

weekend to cook up enough food for Kazys for the coming week. The commute made her life so difficult that she continued to have the frightening heart palpitation episodes that had started in Hingham. Yet she could not quit her job in Gillette. The company offered an attractive health insurance program for both employees and their spouses that continued into retirement, as a supplement to Medicare. She carried father on her policy, but in order to keep him eligible, she had to work four more years to meet the minimum requirement. It seems that father did not know about this time requirement, when, against mother's protests, he built the house in Manomet. As soon as the four years were up, on April 1, 1981, mother retired at age 58½.

We four children had gone our separate ways, and sad to say, there was only one more time when we all came together. This last meeting, when all four of us were present, occurred in celebration of Dana and Algis' 40th birthday, in August 1987, on Cape Cod. The parents had rented a vacation house in Cape Cod in which we all gathered. Rimas was living in New Hampshire at that time, not far from Algis. With a great act of will power, he had overcome his alcohol and drug addictions. He and Algis drove down together, Dana arrived from Boston, and I flew in from Cincinnati. To commemorate the special occasion, mother gave each of us a small gift, a metal sculpture of a bird on a wooden base. As she handed the birds to us, she said sadly, "My little birds have flown away, but don't forget that you all came from the same nest." The last photograph taken of us four together shows us holding the birds. Today, my bird sits on a shelf behind my bed reminding me daily of the precious memories we share. Dana, too, still treasures her bird, but the boys somehow lost theirs.

Cousins Thomas, Laura and Alex getting into the computer age. Cincinnati, 1989.

Rimas, on a rare visit to the parents in Manomet, along with Algis in 1978.

In 1987 most of the family was on the east coast and we took the opportunity to get together. Here are Rimvydas, Danutė, Algis, Ginny, Alex and Laura on the stairs of the Lithuanian church in South Boston.

Rimas, his daughter Kristina, and Algis in NH; 1980.

Celebrating the twins' 40th birthday (1987) on Cape Cod with Algis' two children, Laura and Alex.

Rimvydas' 48th birthday, October 1993. One of his last photos.

Edvardas Bolisas and Irena Baranauskaitė on their trip to the USA enjoy Chinese food with Audra and Klaus. Cincinnati, 1988.

The Willekes and the parents visited Lithuania together in 1988.

Edita Bolisaitė in Floridas with Rimas' daughter Kris and Audra; 1991.

Jadvyga and Kazys, at their Florida home, repeating their marriage vows after 50 years. March 1993.

Alex and Laura in Laconia, NH.

Edmundas Reklaitis' family.

Kazys and Jadvyga at their
Florida home at Christmas time.

Jadvyga singing in chorus, "Sietynas," in Ormond Beach. She is second from left.

The Jepsen family (Katherine, Paul, Kris, Donny) and
Dana welcome Jadvyga when she moves from Florida to
Pembroke in 2009.

Jadvyga, with Antanelis Bolis
(son of her brother Antanas) at her
father's grave in Alytus in 2000.

Audra with cousin Antanėlis Bolisas and wife Regina. Alytus, 2013.

Vytas and Claire getting to know cousin Gražina and her husband, Antanas Lingis, in Vilnius; 2013.

Audra and Laimutė Bolisaitė in Kėdainiai, 2013.

Algis and Dalė wed on February 14, 1999.

Flowers surround mother on her last Mother's Day at Dana's in 2012.

Celebrating mother's 90th birthday with her grandchildren: Kristina, Vytas and Laura. Alex was unable to come.

Chapter XII: The Florida Years

While mother had disliked the isolation and inconvenience of the Manomet house, she was enthusiastic about the move to Florida. This came about unexpectedly and was a disappointment for Dana who had moved back from Germany to be closer to the parents. Klaus, Vytas and I frequently left Cincinnati for warmer climates during Christmas or spring breaks. We went to Cancun, Mexico, several times, and also to Florida. While we were planning such a trip to Florida, I invited our parents to join us in Juno Beach. Their first vacation in Florida proved to be decisive — they wanted to live there.

We had settled comfortably in Manomet. I had even built a greenhouse that attached to the house — it was like a miniature farm. I had not expected to live anywhere else, but it turned out differently. Prior to Christmas 1981, Audronė told us she and her family were going to Florida and suggested that we spend the holidays there together. We had never been to Florida, so we accepted this idea gladly. When we flew out of Massachusetts, we left behind a cold, snowy winter. Arriving in Florida we found a warm, pleasant summer. We were able to swim and enjoy the sun every day. In other words, Florida enchanted us — those two weeks passed by like a beautiful dream. Returning home we started to think: why should we shovel snow and suffer through cold winters, when not far away is a land of eternal summer. Next winter, in January 1983, we again went down to Florida, this time with our own car. Arriving in Juno Beach we started to look into buying a house. It turned out, however, that houses close to the beach were too expensive for us, while further away from the ocean it was too hot in the summer. The same was true for building lots. Southern Florida was already densely populated, so we had to give up on Juno Beach.

Kazys enjoyed his retirement years in Florida.

On our drive home, we stopped to visit our friends, the Ambrozaitis, who had recently built a house in Ormond Beach. Just then, not far from them, a new development called Seabridge South had opened and the lots were very inexpensive. From the available 104 lots we chose one we liked best and purchased it for $18,600, including all fees. The area was attractive and close to the ocean. Once I had the lot, how could I let it stand vacant? At home, in the course of the summer, I prepared the plans for the new house

Happy by the water in Ormond Beach, Florida.

and when we returned to Florida in October 1983, we started to build. We found temporary quarters in an empty house close by that belonged to our friend Dr. Majauskas. We finished construction and moved in on February 2, 1984. We sold the Manomet house at the end of January 1985 with all the furniture and other inventory. We brought with us only the most essential belongings; all other furnishings we bought here in Florida.

We are happy that we left the cold, snowy north and moved to this land of eternal summer and sunshine, where flowers bloom all year. We found here a small but active Lithuanian community that we joined right away. Jadzė sings in a choir called "Sietynas" [The Pleiades], while I frequently provide the readings and recitations of poetry at our celebrations. Around us we have good neighbors and quite a few friends. There's never time to be bored — we are always occupied with some activity. We live without any great worries and still enjoy good health. For all this we thank God. We don't plan to move anywhere else, only to our place of "eternal rest" that we have already purchased in the Volusia Memorial Park, Section E-3, Lot 233, spaces 1 and 2. The moving dates are still uncertain — only God knows them.

My memoir tells the story of my generation. This generation was destined to live through a stormy and difficult period of history: two world wars, military occupations, loss of freedom, terrible slavery under communism, the flight from *our country, and the struggle to gain a foothold in a foreign land.*

I will soon be 76 years old, not a short lifespan. As I look back at the life that has passed (so quickly), what can I say briefly about myself? God's guiding hand has led me through all the storms and dangers, without major misfortune. He gave me a fine wife, good, healthy children and grandchildren. He gifted me with good health and some talents. For my part, whatever I tackled, I attempted to complete as well as I could, to the best of my understanding. Wherever I lived, I tried to improve and beautify my surroundings, so as to leave the world a bit better and more attractive. The Highest Judge will decide whether I succeeded.

With this I conclude my story. I hope my children will complete the narrative of my life when they write their own memoirs.

Kazys Barūnas
38 Sand Dollar Drive
Ormond Beach, Florida 32074
January 20, 1988

Kazys ended his memoir in 1988 as though his story were concluded. But there was much more to come — his life was far from over. He lived another 19 years and experienced many joyful and tragic events. He died just short of his 95th birthday.

1988 was an eventful year, both for our parents and for Lithuanians around the world. That summer, the flag of independent Lithuania — yellow, green, and red stripes — flew once again over Gediminas Castle in Vilnius and people took to the streets in mass demonstrations against Soviet rule. Our parents were there in Vilnius to witness these momentous events. They were witnesses to the beginning of the peaceful struggle that led to Lithuania's independence in 1990 and marked the end of the Soviet Union. Klaus and I had decided to travel to Lithuania that summer of 1988 and to take 14-year-old Vytas along. Klaus suggested that I ask my parents if they wanted to come with us. I predicted that father would say no: he had always said he'd never go back to Lithuania as long as it was under Soviet rule. Much to my surprise, when I proposed the visit, he and mother said yes immediately. In order to feel more secure, they signed up to travel with a tour group of American Lithuanians on a two-week visit. Klaus and I planned our trip independently, out of Cincinnati, and we stayed longer. We met up with our parents in Lithuania, as planned, and witnessed the emotional reunions with their relatives whom they had not seen since 1944. All of mother's five brothers were deceased but she still had her sister Stefa and cousin Zosė, both living in Kaunas, as well as numerous nephews and nieces. Our father found two siblings still living, brother Petras and sister Damutė, along with nephews, nieces, and pre-war friends. Jadvyga and Kazys were eager to see the places of their youth again, to visit their family graves. So much had changed in the intervening years — it was both joyful and painful to be there.

They were astonished to witness the first meetings of "Sajudis" (The Movement), an organization like Lech Walesa's "Solidarity" in Poland, whose purpose was to regain self-rule for Lithuania. Initially, the younger generation of Communist leaders in Lithuania, emboldened by Mikhail Gorbachev's call for "perestroika" (restructuring) and "glasnost" (openness), demanded that the Lithuanian Soviet Socialist Republic have more local autonomy. But soon "Sajudis" was taken over by the general population led by Vytautas Landsbergis, a fearless professor of music. Landsbergis would not stop at anything short of complete independence for Lithuania. His goal was: let's throw the occupiers out of our country! In the summer of 1988 it was not clear

Mother stands at the entrance to the former Red Cross Hospital in Kaunas where she trained as a nurse.

how these political developments would evolve, but Kazys and Jadvyga were filled with hope. They had never expected to see such a change in their lifetime. The Soviet Union had seemed all-powerful. Suddenly the Lithuanian national flag flew above Gediminas Castle, and not just one — hundreds appeared, big and small. Where did all those flags come from? Had someone been sewing and storing them secretly? The hatred of the Lithuanian population for the Soviet system was out in the open and could never again be concealed.

While in Lithuania, Kazys and Jadvyga invited two relatives, one from each side of the family, to visit the United States. Since Gorbachev's liberalization had started in 1985, such visits had become feasible. Mother invited Edvardas Bolisas, the son of her oldest brother Aleksandras (Olekas), the same Edvardas who had tried to smuggle Klaus and me out of Vilnius in 1969. Olekas had been like a father to his two young sisters, Jadvyga and Stefa, after their father died. Jadvyga felt a life-long gratitude to him, but since he was no longer alive

(d. 1972), she repaid her "debt" by inviting his son. Kazys chose Irena Baranauskaitė, his oldest brother Juozas' daughter and a professor of herbal medicine at Kaunas University. Juozas had provided Kazys with a place to live for two years, while he was studying engineering at the technical college in Kaunas. Since Juozas had died in 1973, Kazys expressed his gratitude via the daughter.

Edvardas and Irena, who hardly knew each other, arrived in Florida in September 1988 and became travel companions for a month. They were excited to see the sandy beaches, the palm trees, Cape Canaveral, Disneyworld, Orlando, and so much more that was new for them. The parents generously footed their travel expenses and also took them shopping. From Florida they traveled to the Boston area to visit with Dana, to New Hampshire to see Algis and his family, then they came to Klaus and me in Cincinnati. It was fun to watch how their eyes opened when they observed life in the United States. Some times the small things captured their attention and made them question their own system. For example, as we drove Edvardas and Irena into a downtown underground garage in Cincinnati to park for the day, Klaus pulled out a ticket at the entrance while a guardrail rose up to let us pass. Edvardas, the construction engineer, asked: "Who makes sure that this guardrail functions? What happens when the mechanism breaks down?" In his experience, a guardrail like that would always be broken and no one would bother to fix it. I took my two cousins on a car trip from Ohio to Michigan to attend a weekend workshop of lectures, readings and discussions organized by a group of Lithuanian American intellectuals. They were amazed by the frankness of the debates, the welcoming, informal atmosphere, and the well-informed discussions about recent events in Lithuania. This was all so new and wonderful for them — a different world. On the drive home, we stopped in a state park to stretch our legs in nature. Again, some of the "small things" they noticed puzzled them. Irena mentioned to me with embarrassment that she needed to use a toilet. I led them to the park toilet building. When we met outside again, Irena and Edvardas could not hide their surprise. The toilets were so clean! They did not smell! There were toilet paper, working faucets, soap, and paper towels in the middle of the woods. They marveled: how does this get done? How come it works so well? They felt like they had come to a different planet.

The year 1993 marked a significant occasion: our parents' 50th wedding anni-versary on March 4. They invited a large group of friends to their home for a celebration and renewal of vows. Klaus, Vytas, and I could not attend for we were spending a sabbatical year (1992–93) in Germany that also included a visit to Lithuania. As an anniversary gift to our parents, we invited them to visit us in

Munich that summer. Vytas, who was criss-crossing Europe that year, arranged to be in Munich to welcome them and do some sightseeing together. We had asked our parents what country or city in Europe they would like to see. They told us: Austria, partic-

Celebrating their 50th wedding anniversary in Austria.

ularly Vienna. The four of us drove along the Danube, stopping to visit splendid baroque churches, castles, palaces, and romantic medieval towns. To mark their anniversary in a special way, Klaus and I planned a surprise for them, something they had not experienced before. Instead of taking them to a restaurant, we brought them to a typical Austrian feast: roast suckling pig and wine served in a tree-shaded garden by waitresses in folk attire. An accordion player strolled around singing traditional romantic songs. Noticing our charming mother across the garden, he sat down at our table, praised her sparking blue eyes and began to serenade her. Mother knew some of the songs and could sing along. It was an enchanting evening.

Rimas' Death

Six months after this happy event, Kazys and Jadvyga experienced perhaps the greatest sorrow in their lives. Rimas died suddenly of a heart attack on January 23, 1994, while working out on a treadmill in a Daytona Beach gym. He had been living with the parents for about half a year. A strange irony of fate occurred that day. Mother was in the hospital visiting an elderly acquaintance; she did not know that at that same time Rimas was brought to the emergency room where efforts were made to revive him — with no success.

Before coming to live with the parents in Ormond Beach, Rimas had lived in New Hampshire for several years, not far from Algis. By then, he was free of alcohol and drugs for about a decade, since 1982. He was glad to be living in nature — he loved the wild beauty of New Hampshire — and he was glad to reconnect with his family. He continued to do hard physical labor, be it woodcutting, mowing grass with a tractor, or factory work, while also attending

Alcoholics Anonymous (AA) and Narcotics Anonymous (NA) meetings regularly. He volunteered in a prison where he counseled prisoners about their addictions. He had created a meaningful life for himself but was not fully satisfied. He dreamed about other possibilities: "Some day I would like to own a bit of land and grow apples and other fruits, heat my house with firewood and solar heat, and make my living working the land... All my life I have daydreamed a lot and still do. These fantasies help me to live in a world that's sometimes cold. And everything comes from within anyway. What we imagine is what we can achieve" (letter to me of October 16,1989). Greeting me with my birthday (January 10, 1990), he reflected on his troubled relationship to his family: "It's good that we remember one another and send each other greetings. I keep feeling closer to the other members of our family. This was not always so during the past forty years and so I feel all kinds of new emotions. I have started to feel 'a part of,' rather than 'apart.'"

Rimas' last Christmas in Ormond Beach, 1993.

In February, 1990 he traveled to Russia and to Lithuania as one of five chaperones for a group of New Hampshire high school students on an exchange program. While in Vilnius, he met with people who wanted to establish chapters of Narcotics Anonymous (NA). He met with doctors in a substance abuse clinic, with patients, with prisoners (addicts), and with the media for a radio interview. He also visited with our relatives in Vilnius. Upon his return to the U.S., he published an account of his experiences in the magazine "Positive Alternatives." In his last message to me, a Christmas card written in December 1993, just weeks before his death, he talked about simplicity: "I've lived very simply for most of my life and have found that simplicity brings its own rewards.... Over the years I've learned to have a little more patience and acceptance of universal laws which bring about my dreams in their own time." At the time of his death, he was on a spiritual path that gave him inner strength — he was drawn to Buddhism and he practiced meditation. Dana had spent that Christmas with the parents and Rimas in Florida. She treasures the last encounter she had with our brother and the prediction he left with her as he dropped her off at the airport. "You will never be rich, but you'll always have what you need."

When news reached us of Rimas' death, Dana, Kristina, and I immediately flew to Florida. For Kris, who had seen so little of her father throughout her life, his death robbed her of the opportunity to reconcile with him and get to know him. A large part of the Daytona Beach Lithuanian community was present at the wake service and funeral to support our parents. Rimas' NA and AA friends came as well and spoke at the wake. A friend of our parents, Juozė Krištolaitytė-Daugėlienė, composed a moving poem and read it at the wake service (January 27, 1994). It was a fitting testament to a life cut short so suddenly and it spoke of a virtue that Rimas had developed in his later years: gentle humility.

The Last Morning

Juozė Krištolaitytė-Daugėlienė

A miraculously beautiful morning —
the sun with wide rays
hovers above the Atlantic's waves;
And the blue of the heavens is
so wide, so deep
my eyes sink into the immeasurable
blue depths.

Seagulls dive by me
waving widely their wings
as if greeting me
and the bright morning.

And I reflect...
reflect on how great and wondrous life is,
how much beauty the Lord's hand
has bestowed on man.

And I, a speck of dust, tiny and insignificant
can delight in all that I see,
that I hear, and that I feel...

You brought me here out of the Unknown,
Oh my Father.
And hold in your hand my existence.
Don't let my days here slide
like on ice into the unknown, into non-existence
and disappear...

And suddenly I hear a voice from a distance
—Son, where are you? Come,
I await you.
I shudder,
but then...
I bow my head obediently
and silently reply
—Oh Father, you're calling me?
I come, I hurry...
Holy is Thy will, oh my Heavenly Father!

[translated from Lithuanian by Dana Barūnas]

In that same momentous year of 1994, Rimas' daughter Kristina married Paul Jepsen on October 15 in a lovely ceremony in Boston. She had met him at a golf club, golf being his passion. Kris, like her "Tėvukas" Kazys, is gifted for all things technical and electronic. She was employed as a computer technician until she started her own business in electronic media. Their daughter Katherine was born on June 22, 1998, in Newton, Massachusetts and son Donald on July 11, 2000, in the same town. Some years later, Kristina and Paul purchased a comfortable home on a large lot in Mansfield, Mass-achusetts, where they cultivate a productive vegetable garden that would make grandfather Kazys proud. Kazys and Jadvyga had lived long enough to know and love their great-grandchildren!

In 1994 as well, Dana built her house in Pembroke, Massachusetts, south of Boston, in an attractive site above a pond, surrounded by pines and oaks. Returning from Germany, she had gone to work in the advertising department of Jordan Marsh, a large department store in downtown Boston. For a while, she rented an apartment in Savin Hill, then moved further south to Hanover, so she could be closer to her beloved horse Ima Speck o Pepper who was stabled there. This horse was "the love of her life" and perhaps reconciled her some-what to her new life, despite the many disappointments she experienced in the United States. When a large corporation bought Jordan Marsh and the advertising department moved to New York, Dana chose not to move but rather to set out on her own as a freelance graphic designer. The house she built in Pembroke was well suited for this independent life. She designed an office for herself and acquired the needed equipment. In her walkout basement she planned a large studio apartment that Algis

Dana and Speck having the time of their lives.

helped to construct. This apartment was intended for the parents — a place where they could spend a portion of every summer to escape the Florida heat. And, thinking ahead, it was a place where Jadvyga could come to live, if she were left a widow. This was a likely scenario, since Kazys was almost eleven years older.

Not long after Rimas' death, Algis left New Hampshire and came to stay with the parents in Ormond Beach. His marriage had been failing for some time and ended in divorce. In Florida he started a new life, finding various jobs in an area that had few jobs to offer. He met and married (February 14, 1999) Dalė Žindžytė Andrijauskienė who had arrived recently from

Father at Dana's newly-built house, stands by the hemlock he just planted. It grew to be about 30 feet tall.

Kaunas to work in the United States. She brought with her a young son, Andrius, a gifted student who went on to earn advanced degrees in engineering. For the parents, having Algis and Dalė close by was a big support, especially after Kazys' health started to fail.

In spite of the emotional blow from Rimas' death, Kazys and Jadvyga continued to live active lives. The independence movement that he had witnessed in Lithuania in 1988 energized Kazys. It became the purpose of his life to help the movement in whatever way he could. He wrote letters to U.S. local and national politicians, published letters to the editor in American and Lithuanian papers; he organized political meetings among the Lithuanians in Daytona Beach and donated money to Sajudis. He became fully absorbed by politics: reading newspapers, watching the news

Algis and Dalė, his second wife, who came from Lithuania.

on TV, following the events with complete attention, and discussing the latest developments with like-minded friends. He even made sure we, his children, applied for and received Lithuanian passports. After Lithuania achieved full independence, our parents visited again. Father took Algis with him on a trip in 1998. The highlight of this visit was a private interview with the then president of Lithuania, Valdas Adamkus, who was aware of our father's political activities. The following year, mother traveled with Dana. In addition to Vilnius, Kaunas and the coast, the two of them visited the small town of Kėdainiai where Jadvyga was born. While Dana returned home after two weeks, mother stayed a full month, spending an extended period of time with her sister Stefa.

Algis and Father met President Valdas Adamkus while in Vilnius in 1998. Father said he gave the Lithuanian president some good advice.

Kazys and Jadvyga enjoyed their lives in Florida. They participated in the Lithuanian community of Daytona Beach; father tended his garden, mother volunteered for several organizations. She delivered meals to the elderly with Meals on Wheels, then worked at a parish thrift shop, a volunteer job she loved. Here she met friendly American women who appreciated her and called her Heidi (Jadvyga = Hedwig = Heddy, and that sounds like Heidi). She enjoyed buying and bringing home inexpensive "treasures" from the shop. There she found all the clothes for father and herself; she even mailed packages — linens, towels — to Dana and me, all from her thrift shop! She had fun while doing good work: raising money for the poor of the parish. The parents received visitors frequently; their children, grandchildren, and great-grandchildren came to see them, especially during the holidays, and were warmly welcomed. They also continued to travel: to Cincinnati to visit Vytas, Klaus, and me and to Pembroke to spend a part of each summer with Dana. In August 1997 the family gathered in Pembroke to celebrate Dana and Algis' 50th birthday — a gala event. They flew to California in 1997 to attend Vytas' graduation from Stanford University. He received a Bachelor of Arts degree in Symbolic Systems. From California, Kazys, Jadvyga, Vytas, Klaus, and I flew to Portland, Oregon, where Klaus' sister Ingrid and her husband Thomas Palm hosted a family celebration in Vytas' honor. Jadvyga had incredible luck playing pool in the Palm's basement, while her fans cheered her on. Both she and Kazys fell in love with the beautiful scenery of the Northwest. As mentioned before, they traveled to Lithuania once more, Kazys with Algis in 1998 and Jadvyga with Dana in 1999. After Klaus and I bought a house in Orinda, California, in 2000, the parents were still well enough to visit us several times.

October 5, 2002 — Jadvyga's 80th birthday! She did not expect anyone to make a big fuss about it, but the family decided to prepare a celebration. Klaus and I rented a large house in Orlando, Florida, with five bedrooms and a swimming pool. Mother, father, Algis, and Dalė arrived by car. Dana, Kristina, Klaus and I flew in. By delightful coincidence, Edita Bolisaitė, our cousin Edvardas' daughter, was visiting the United States and was able to join us. We cooked together, laughed, ate, soaked in the pool, and

Celebrating mother's 80th birthday in Orlando, with special guest, cousin Edita (center), visiting from Kaunas.

visited a water park. It was a joy to be together on such an occasion. The big surprise was a slide show, with music, that Kris had created to illustrate mother's life. We were touched to see the old photos and appreciated Kris' creativity.

Mother's 80th birthday, playing in the private pool at the rented house in Orlando.

Kazys and Jadvyga loved the home they had built in Ormond Beach, the beautifully landscaped garden, the "eternal" Florida summers, their Lithuanian friends, and their friendly American neighbors. They took a walk every evening around the circular street that made up their neighborhood and stopped to chat with the many people they knew. They enjoyed walking along the beach; in later years, they just stood on the shore and looked down at the waves. They had earned their long retirement and they savored every bit of it.

Our parents loved living in Florida and often entertained guests. Here Algis, Dalė and Dalė's aunt.

Conclusion: The Cycle of Life

We are all aware that we are subject to the biological cycle of life: birth, growth, maturity, old age, and death. In addition to this physical cycle, I believe there is a corresponding inner desire to return to one's origins. In youth, we eagerly dash off to seek our own adventures, to escape the limitations of the family circle, to see the world, to test our strength, and to form our own family units. In maturity and old age, we begin to evaluate and reflect on the world of our youth, our family, and our ancestry. We desire to mentally revisit that past, those places and people we left behind in order to take stock and to understand ourselves — the spiritual task of aging. We reconsider our past in memoirs, in poetry, in the questions we ask and the information we seek. I don't know if this is a universal phenomenon but it's one that I have observed in myself and in many of those around me. Sometimes this spiritual return "home" may not be fully conscious — it just "happens."

Klaus and I led active and fulfilling lives in Cincinnati, where we lived for 26 years. He established a successful laboratory for aerosol science in the Department of Environmental Health at the University of Cincinnati, with scientists and graduate students who came from around the world. He was awarded tenure, was promoted to full professor, and received numerous awards for his teaching and his publications. I taught German language and literature in the Department of German, Russian, and East Asian Languages at Miami University, also chairing that department for five years. I too was awarded tenure and promoted to full professor. While most of my research focused on German literature (the early 20th century), I was also drawn to Lithuanian literature; I began to publish articles on it and to participate in Baltic Studies organizations. Klaus and I continued our contacts with Lithuania throughout the Soviet era; these intensified and became easier after independence in 1990. In a sense, Klaus "adopted" Lithuania. As a gift to me for our 25th wedding anniversary in 1993, he determined to learn Lithuanian — a difficult undertaking because it is so different from the West European languages he already knew. He studied valiantly and achieved some ability to read and to converse. This greatly impressed Lithuanians who don't expect "outsiders" to learn their archaic and difficult language. We visited Lithuania in 1992 and again in 1998, both times with Vytas. Klaus brought a number of scientists to his lab from Lithuania, then obtained a NATO grant to fund collaboration with Lithuanian scientists in environmental research. He traveled to Lithuania a number of times without me, in connection with this research.

My youthful desire to escape the world of my parents had been temporary. I see now that my entire life has been marked by my Lithuanian heritage and traditions. The seeds planted by our parents with love and longing continued to flourish in their children, even in their partners and grandchildren.

Our time spent together in California in the 1960s had been golden years. The West Coast continued to beckon us, but until we were ready to retire, we were bound to our academic jobs in the Midwest. We spent our last sabbatical year (2000–2001) in the San Francisco Bay area and that experience rekindled our desire to return to our first joint "home." Somewhat prematurely, we bought our house in Orinda in the fall of 2000, while still on sabbatical and with continued obligations to our research projects and universities in Ohio. In retrospect, this turned out to be one of the best decisions we ever made. Vytas found his way back to California soon after us. Having earned a Master's degree from Stanford University in computer science, specializing in robotics, he took his first job in Pittsburgh, Pennsylvania to work on an innovative mobile robots project. However, two years in the Midwest were enough for him. Back in California he found a position with a robotics group at the National Aeronautics and Space Administration (NASA) in Sunnyvale. In 2005, he married Claire Rose, a genuine Californian, born and raised in San Diego.; They settled in the Mission District of San Francisco, just a short train ride away from us. At the same time that he changed his name from Thomas to Vytas, our son and his wife created a new family name for themselves: the SunSpirals.

Vytas and Claire's wedding, 2005.

Kazys' Death

After age 90, Kazys' health began to decline, although for his age he remained quite energetic. He took daily walks, supporting himself with a cane, and continued to look after his garden. As he relied more on mother, he began to pay attention to her opinions and realized how competent she was. Until then, he alone had made most of the major decisions. Now he asked for her advice. The last two years of his life were marred by pain, a series of ailments and medical emergencies. In 2005, at 93, Kazys suffered a heart attack and was hospitalized for three weeks. When I visited him in the hospital, he seemed pessimistic; he was too weak to get up from the bed

Father regaining strength in rehab (2005), with visiting granddaughter Kristina.

alone and doubted he would get well or go home again. I chased down his doctor and asked for a frank prognosis. The doctor told me that he expected father to survive, and, after a stay in a rehabilitation facility, he could regain enough strength to go home. I returned to father's bedside and asked him whether he was still interested in living. He said, yes, he continued to be curious about life and eager to share in the lives of his children, grandchildren, and great-grandchildren. I reported what the doctor said, assured him that a stay in a rehab facility would be temporary, just until he could stand up and walk a bit by himself. Then he could go back home into mother's good care. He took this message to heart, and, always strong-willed, he worked with the therapists to regain his strength. Throughout his hospitalization and therapy, Jadvyga, Algis, and Dalė visited him daily, bringing homemade soup and other goodies to boost his health and morale. The effort paid off — he lived at home for another year and a half, until his final hospitalization in February 2007.

As a trained nurse, Jadvyga cared for Kazys with skill and dedication, but the non-stop problems exhausted her. The last eighteen months were the most difficult. She herself was now over 80, an age when most people lose stamina and require some support. Both she and Kazys were fearful of ending their days in a nursing home — she did everything to avoid such a fate for father. He lived in his own home until his final hospitalization. Fortunately, his mind remained clear to the end. On the day before he was rushed to the hospital for the last time, he cleared his desk, writing the last check, to save mother that burden. Klaus and I received the call that father was on his deathbed while in San Miguel, Mexico, where we had planned to spend the month of February. Klaus immediately booked a flight for me to Florida. I arrived at the hospital in Daytona Beach in time to say farewell to him. Mother, Algis and Dalė were also by his bedside when he passed away on February 9. The cause of death was recorded as congestive heart failure. Dana, Kristina, Vytas, Claire, and Klaus arrived for the wake service and funeral. At the wake, the two grandchildren recounted, with deep emotion, what their grandfather had meant to them — what they had learned from him. With great sadness we buried him in the grave he had chosen for himself, next to Rimas. He had lived a full and meaningful life to the end. His great joy toward the end of his life was to witness Lithuania independent once more and to return to his origins, to visit the graves of his ancestors.

Jadvyga Continues Alone

Jadvyga, suddenly alone after 64 years of marriage, was exhausted and depressed. She had put so much energy into nursing Kazys — now what was she to do? He had taken care of all the paperwork, the bills and the bank accounts. She felt helpless facing the many bureaucratic tasks that a death brings. I stayed an additional two weeks to help her sort through and complete the paperwork. She learned quickly. In the two years that she lived alone in Ormond Beach, she developed many new skills: how to write a check, how to balance a bank account, how to organize her paperwork in a file, how to take care of the garden, and much more. She took pride in being able to manage on her own but became increasingly tired. She developed a frequent cough that her doctor could not diagnose — he assumed it was an allergy — and that deprived her of strength. Finally, she decided it was time to return north, to accept Dana's constant urging to live with her in Pembroke, in the studio apartment prepared for her many years ago. Dana visited her in February, 2009 to start packing, and in March I came to Ormond Beach to

Mother arrived in Pembroke, to her new home, in March 2009. She lived there for almost 4 years.

help her sell the house, pack, and move. The many happy years in Florida had come to an end and mother calmly accepted the new reality. She sensed that soon she would not be able to live on her own; she would need help. Letting go of material possessions was easy for her. What she treasured was her family.

The situation for Jadvyga in Pembroke was ideal. She had her own separate space in the studio apartment that she knew from many visits. Familiar things surrounded her: furniture, paintings, photos and her car. She could lead an independent existence, yet she was never alone, because Dana, who works from home as a graphic designer, was a daily companion. Mother was eager to be helpful — she drove to the grocery store, prepared dinner, did some light work in the garden. Dana involved her in her life as much as mother desired. They periodically drove down to South Boston to attend Mass at the old Lithuanian parish and to meet acquaintances. They stopped at the Lithuanian Club for home-cooked food. Dana took her on local excursions: to the beach, to parks, to see the house in Manomet. When Dana had visitors, Jadvyga was invited to join. She attended events at the senior center in Pembroke, read avidly, watched television, wrote letters and cards, made phone calls to Florida and to her sister Stefa in Lithuania. She lived a full and active life for two years in Pembroke, until her health began to fail.

During the entire time mother lived in Pembroke, Dana's friend Bruce Nickerson was a wonderful support. Dana and Bruce had been friends as students at the Massachusetts College of Art, which they both attended in the 1960s. Many years later, they reconnected; Bruce became a part of Dana's life and an "adopted" member of our family. He was right there when Dana needed assistance in some aspect of caring for mother; he helped to make her life comfortable. He has been a welcome participant in our family

Danguolė, from Kaunas, took wonderful care of mother in her final year. Audra visited frequently from California.

celebrations and sorrows.

Mother had a knack for knowing the right time to do things. Although she enjoyed driving and loved her little Corolla, she decided to give it up. She made this decision without any sentimentality or complaint about the loss of independence it would bring. No one had to pry the car keys out of her hands, as sometimes

Mother loved visits from her grandchildren, as here with Alex.

happens with elderly people. She herself recognized and accepted the new reality, apologizing to Dana that she would now have to drive for both of them. Mother had numerous ailments that lead to her decline. Osteoporosis caused spinal fractures that gave her severe back pain. She underwent surgery to fuse that area of the spine — this provided little relief. When she fell in her room, she broke her hip, and again needed surgery to replace the hip. Months of physical therapy followed, and a difficult recovery. With Dana's persistence and

The family gathered to celebrate mother's 90th birthday. She was so happy.

encouragement, she managed to come home again and to walk. The twin diseases that ended her life were chronic obstructive pulmonary disease (COPD) and a cancer of the red blood cells (myelodysplastic syndrome). Although mother never smoked, her lungs may have been compromised by years of breathing fiber dust in the sewing factory. She now needed constant oxygen assistance, both at home and in the car. The blood cancer made her anemic and also decreased the oxygen available to her body. This disease could only be managed with regular blood transfusions that became more and more frequent.

In order to take care of mother at home, Dana arranged for visiting nurses and physical therapists. She obtained the equipment necessary to make home nursing feasi-

Jadvyga's 90th birthday celebration. On the left Donny and Kristina and some old friends on the right.

ble: a hospital bed, commode, wheelchairs, and much more. When mother could no longer be left alone, she hired part-time nursing assistants. Finally, when 24-hour care became necessary, she found a woman from Lithuania to live in the house and help full time. This wonderful woman was Danguolė Buivydytė from Kaunas who took care of our mother with love and became a friend of the family.

Although in constant pain, mother expressed again and again how fortunate she was to be surrounded by love and to be in her own home. Her life shrank to a small circle of daily activities. She especially enjoyed sitting on her flower-filled patio in good weather, soaking up the sun, and watching the birds at the feeders. Dana made sure there were always seeds in the feeders, flowers blooming on the patio, and a fresh bouquet in mother's room. These were her simple daily joys. Her big joys were the phone calls from Algis and Dalė in Florida and from me from California, and also the visits from all of us, from her grandchildren, and great-grandchildren. Kristina frequently brought Donny and Katherine to spend time with Močiute. Algis' daughter Laura, in medical school, training to become an oral surgeon, took time to visit from Philadelphia. Her brother Alex came from New York City where he worked for an advertising agency. Vytas and Claire flew in from California. These young people, all leading busy lives, found time to visit Močiute and to express their love.

A big day for Jadvyga and the whole family was the celebration of her 90th birthday in October 2012. As many of the family as could come were there for this weekend event. On Sunday morning, neighbors and friends arrived to greet her. The table was set for brunch; there was champagne, singing, cards, flowers, and presents to open. Mother even received a congratulatory card from President Obama! Her blue eyes sparkling, smiling, she asked in amazement: "Is this all for me?"

Jadvyga's Death

Mother may have set herself the goal to reach her 90th birthday because the end came so soon after that. She died at home at 5 am on November 29, 2012. Dana had called me two days before to tell me that mother would not last long. I talked to mother one more time on the phone to tell her I loved her and would be coming to her. She understood but could no longer respond in words, only sounds. The morning I was to fly, Dana called with the sad news that she had died, especially sad for me because I wanted to be with her in her last moments. On the way to Boston, my heart bursting with sorrow, I wrote a poem that tried to express what she meant to me.

BUT DEATH WOULD NOT WAIT
In Memory of My Mother, Jadvyga Barūnas

Mamyte, I'm coming soon, but not just now.
After Thanksgiving, when flying is easier.
I say, aš tave labai myliu.
You whisper into the phone, a word, a sigh… no longer able to speak.
Our last communication.
Mamyte, I'm coming, but not today.
I boil the turkey bones for the broth,
Wash the guest linen.
A yoga class to stretch me out for sitting in the plane.
The house is in order, the suitcase packed.
I'm flying tomorrow, Mamyte, to be at your side,
To hold your hand when you draw your last breath.
To whisper last words of love in your ear.
But death would not wait.

It snuck in at night and stole your last breath.
It laughed at my orderly house, my packed suitcase.
Now my vocabulary is poorer.
For the sweet word Mamytė has lost its use.

To whom will I say it?
The affectionate form of my name, Audrutė, rings in my ears-
But who will speak it?
I longed to see your blue eyes once more,
But death would not wait.
I am an orphan,
No longer a daughter to anyone.

There is much to be said about my mother's life,
But who will want to hear it?
The bomb shelters, the hunger, the fear?
Years in DP camps: there she buried her mother in foreign soil.
Four children to be washed, fed, comforted.
Who comforted her for her losses?
Photos of my father, emaciated, surviving on onion soup and oats.
But the children got fed somehow.
In German meadows, my mother young and beautiful,
Among the refugees, celebrating spring and their own survival.

Who wants to hear about her work in a factory?
Years of rushing home with bags of groceries in her arms.
In the kitchen, the sounds of onions sizzling and laughter.
I peel potatoes, Dana sets the table
Dinner's ready for father when he comes home from work.
Mother takes pride in that.
Who wants to hear about the anguish she felt
When Rimas disappeared?
Now and then a word from Alberta, or was it Utah?
He's working on an oilrig, in construction; he's still alive!
Who can imagine her pain the day he died?
In his prime, free of alcohol at last, reclaiming his life.
And still she sang, a soaring soprano,
She sang out her heart in praise of life and her faith.

The even measure of her days in Florida,
Never demanding, always welcoming signs of affection, visits
From her scattered children and grandchildren.
The hot soup waiting after my flights from Ohio or California,
Kindness and joy written on her face.
Amazed that she meant so much to me.

Pride in my accomplishments, whatever they were.
Years of nursing our father, and she over eighty.
How much she learned as a widow: how to pay bills,
How to fix the sprinkler system, her obsession with the grass...
To keep the garden as nice as Daddy did.

Full circle: a return to Massachusetts for her final years.
Meals to prepare, a bit of work in the garden;
Nice to do the laundry... it smells so good.
Pleased she can still be of use, help Dana.
Pride in her grandchildren Vytas, Kris, Laura, Alex:
Grown up and good people.
Her delight in the youngest: Katherine and Donny.
How they hug their Močiutė.
Not a woman of many words, what she thinks and feels is private.
She has her opinions but does not push them, does not argue.
Wisdom in few words.

Who wants to hear how her life shrank to a point?
Her room, her flowers, the birds.
Contented hours on the patio soaking up the sun.
Today she's happy: Algis called from Florida! He's OK.
The tables have turned on her — a sad destiny.
For one used to tending others, she now needs constant care.
Dana her loving caregiver — days of pain, hospitals, blood transfusions.
No complaints, a ready smile, blue eyes shining.
Her favorite word: ačiu, thank you, gratitude for each small service.
In October, her 90th birthday: how much pleasure in the cards,
The family and friends who gather.
"Is this all for me?" she asks, humbled by the attention.
For her California young ones she sings her last song,
"Plaukia sau laivelis..."
With lungs that have forgotten how to breathe.
A few days before the end, "I still want to live," she says.
But death would not wait.

Is this all there is to my mother's life?
So many gaps, so many omissions!
The texture of her life was rough:
Poverty in childhood, work, duty, no room for self-indulgence.

Through my children I have seen the world, she says.
California in the 60s: the Spanish charm of Santa Barbara,
The roller coaster hills of San Francisco.
Oh my! The topless go go bars of North Beach.
Her relief: the singers wear clothes, sing arias.
I'll never believe you again, she scolds.
Klaus and his pranks!
Her eyes wide at the magic of Swan Lake in Music Hall.
Her trips to Europe: with Dana in Munich and Rome.
The roast piglet banquet in Vienna with Klaus and me
To celebrate their 50th anniversary.
An enamored Austrian sings to her blue eyes
While Daddy smiles indulgently.
Her return to Lithuania—she kisses the earth, grateful!
Sister Stefa, Cousin Zosė, grown old and apart—
No longer the same language.
She says, "I have seen so much."
Little was a lot in her life.
I still have Mamytė on my lips
But to whom can I say it?
For Death did not wait.

Written by Audra Willeke
While en route to her mother
On November 29, 2012 —
On the day she died.

Jadvyga's funeral Mass was held in her Lithuanian parish church in South Boston on December 8. Since she wanted to be cremated, she and Dana had decided earlier to purchase a joint vault in the Pembroke town cemetery. The interment of the ashes took place on April 18, 2013 in a small ceremony that Dana described eloquently in an email to the family:

Hi family,
Today we had beautiful weather for our farewell to Močiute. Kris came with the kids [Donny and Katherine] and Jane [Kris Jepsen's mother-in-law]; Bruce [Nickerson] was here, too. I put the Lithuanian soil in the urn with her ashes, along with a rosary that was there and a little angel pin I put on the velvet bag. I put her photo on top of the wall along with her urn and then said my good-byes. I'll attach the little tribute I had written up in advance. I found it hard

to read. Then I read a few verses that "Audrutė" wrote on her last flight out here. Kris said only a few words in Lithuanian and Bruce said good-bye too. Everyone else just had tears in their eyes. [...]

Bruce took the photo of our last good-bye to mother/močiute on April 18, 2013.

I know you were with us in spirit. I'm glad I have done this now. I feel some relief. She would have loved this day, with flowers popping up everywhere and birds chirping. It's a lovely cemetery, with a pretty view where the wall is. But I'm glad I have some of her ashes here. [...]

Love you all,

Dana

Dana's farewell at the Pembroke Cemetery on April 18, 2013, captures the essence of our mother's personality so well that I repeat it here.

Brangi mamyte, močiute,
Šiandien atsisveikinu su Tavim, nors Tu visados būsi su manim — mano širdyje ir mano celėse. Aš Tave labai, labai myliu, amžinai.
[Dear mother, močiute,
Today I say farewell to you, although you will always remain with me, in my heart and in my cells.
I love you very, very much, forever.]

My sweet, beautiful mamyte, it is such a great loss to me not to have you physically in my house anymore. Of course you're still in my heart, where you will stay 'til I die. Some of your ashes are also on my mantle in that beautiful wooden urn I bought from a local artist.
You were always so kind and caring, so generous with all you had. You didn't get angry or in a bad mood, even when you were in pain the last two years; you tried not to complain. You were so grateful for any little thing people did for you and you thanked them always. But those were just the declining years.

I recall how charming you were among your friends and acquaintances. I was always proud to have such a beautiful mother. Everyone liked you, and if they didn't, it was because they were jealous of your beauty, your personality, your voice and talents. When my friends would sometimes complain about their mothers, I would say, sorry, I can't bitch about my mom. She's wonderful. They agreed.

You never cared about material things, sharing what you had with your sister in Lithuania, helping relatives, including your children and grandchildren, for decades. I remember how you would keep it from Tėvukas so he wouldn't know how much you gave away each month. You said it was money you earned and you would spend it as you wished — on others.

You always smiled and everyone smiled back. You constantly brought cake or candy to your doctors and never remained "in debt" to anyone who ever helped you.

Your voice was your joy. It was so beautiful. I remember you singing as you prepared dinner in the kitchen in Savin Hill. It was a constant, beautiful sound. I wonder how you had the energy and joy to sing after a long day working in the sweatshops, or the assembly belt at Gillette, coming home, carrying heavy bags of groceries on the ten-minute walk from the train station. You didn't bother to ask the boys to help you. After making dinner you would maybe sew a new dress or go to choir

Putting mother's ashes on her father's grave in Alytus.

practice and you always had time for us. It was a long tiring day, but you stayed upbeat throughout, never complaining.

When I think about becoming a better person, I think of you. You are my heroine.

It's a wonder you stayed so good after all the hardships you endured. Though it did make you a bit mistrusting and suspicious of people you didn't know well. I think I was your best friend — you trusted me with all you had, including your life. I hope I didn't make too many mistakes in my care of you. I wish I could

still be caring for you, no matter the stress and fatigue. You didn't want to be a
burden to me, but I'd rather still have you by my side. It's much more of a burden
to lose you.

Good-bye my dearest friend. Rest in Peace.
Sudievu mano drauge, ilsėkis ramiai amžinybėj.

While Jadvyga said that she did not care where her ashes went after her death, for us who survive it seemed fitting to return some part of her to Florida, where she had lived long and happily. Father had already inscribed her name and birth date on the plaque on his grave. Algis and Dalė arranged to have her date of death added. They buried some of her ashes at the gravesite, to join Kazys and Rimas. I decided to return some of her ashes to Lithuania at the first opportunity. This occurred when I learned of a family reunion planned by the Baranauskas side of the family for May 2013. A younger generation, the children of our cousins, initiated this event. Klaus and I spent the second half of May in Lithuania, and, much to our delight, Vytas and Claire decided to join us. Since this visit may be our last, it was a perfect opportunity to pass the baton to our children, to have them make their own contacts in Lithuania. The highlight of the trip was the family reunion on the weekend of May18–19 that took place close to Žaunieriškiai, the village where the Baranauskas family originated. Our first stop on the way to the meeting place was in the cemetery of Alytus. Here Jadvyga's father, Antanas Bolisas, was laid to rest in 1930 when she was a child of eight. And here, it seemed to me, would be the right place to leave some of her ashes. My cousin Antanas Bolisas (the son of mother's brother Antanas) with his wife Regina met us at the cemetery to lead us to our grandfather's grave. How surprised we were to find the grave had been especially prepared for our visit, with lilies-of-the-valley planted on it. Antanas and Regina had traveled to Alytus the day before to do this kind deed. It was a pleasant task to reunite mother's ashes with this earth, a great sense of closure.

The family reunion, about thirty people of all ages, convened with a mass at the parish church of Rumbonys, just a few miles from the Baranauskas homestead in Žaunieriškiai. This was the church where Kazys was baptized, where he walked to Sunday services. The burial ground behind the church is a traditional one, with graves spread out under ancient trees. We placed flowers and candles on the ancestral graves and gathered for a moment of silent prayer. We found the graves of Kazys' grandfather Jurgis, his father Antanas, and two siblings: sister Teofilė and brother Adomas. I also spotted the grave of father's beloved mentor, the educator Adomas Balynas, about whom Kazys wrote with such respect in his memoir. Outside the church we planted an oak tree with a family plaque and date. May it thrive! After this serious part, the fun began at a country hostel rented for the weekend. The program included music, dancing, games, wonderful food — an atmosphere of

A reunion of the Baranauskas family near the family homestead of Žaunieriškiai, May 2013.

belonging and togetherness. It was a great pleasure to meet the youngest generation, the grandchildren of my cousins, who ran around excitedly under the storks' nest in the courtyard. Vytas' wife Claire, for whom it was a first visit to Lithuania, was welcomed with open arms. She charmed everyone with her natural beauty and grace.

During our stay in Lithuania we were able to reconnect with many of our relatives from both sides of the family. In Vilnius and in Kaunas we spent some time with the cousins and their spouses whom we first met in 1969, with whom we had stayed in touch all these years, across the miles. I was particularly happy to meet for the first time relatives living in Kėdainiai, Jadvyga's birthplace, the descendants of Jadvyga's brother Feliksas. They took Klaus and me on a walk through the town of Kėdainiai, showed us where Jadvyga's father had his workshop, where the family had lived. These buildings are now gone, but most of the town remains unchanged — the same streets and courtyards where little Miss Jadzė walked with the bow in her blond hair. Here too I left her ashes, in the cemetery above the town, on her brother Feliksas' grave. The homecoming was complete, the cycle of life closed.

Kazys had ended his writing in 1988 with the words:

My memoir tells the story of my generation. This generation was destined to live through a stormy and difficult period of history: two world wars, military occupations, loss of freedom, terrible slavery under communism, the flight from our country, and the struggle to gain a foothold in a foreign land.

Now this generation is gone, with few exceptions. A worldview, specific values, and some kinds of knowledge have disappeared along with the passing of these people. This concluding chapter has focused on endings, on the cyclical nature of life that returns to its origins. However, this is not the end of the Barūnas story. We, first generation transplants from Europe, are hyphenated Americans, occupying a sometimes uneasy position between two cultures, feeling like we do not completely belong in either. Our children, the second generation, are no longer hyphenated; they are fully Americans. The Lithuanian roots have dug deep into American soil. May the Barūnas tree continue to flourish in America and may each succeeding generation find strength and inspiration from the struggles of those who have gone before them.

Appendix

Letters sarted arriving from relatives. These are from Kazys' brother, Petras, sent from Siberia. He asked mostly for medications.

The first letter from Kazys' mother arrived in 1947. She dictated her letters to daughter Monika. The last one came, just before she died, in 1965.

First Letter Received from Lithuania after World War II from Kazys' Mother, Magdalena Baranauskienė
Dictated to her daughter Monika on July 10, 1947
Received August 9, 1947, at the DP Camp in Offenbach/Main, Germany

Kazys' mother, Magdalena Kardišauskaitė, born 1883, was the daughter of a prosperous farmer from a village near Alytus. Her marriage to Antanas Baranauskas (about 1900) produced eleven children. She raised them with hard work and much love on a farm that provided the family only bare subsistence. She suffered great loses: three children died in infancy or childhood; of the remaining six sons and two daughters, three sons were lost to her. One died of illness at 35, another son and his family perished in Siberia during World War II, and a third son, Kazys, disappeared with his wife and infant daughter during the war. She learned three years later that he had survived, but she never saw him again. She did not know at the time of writing her letter that yet another son would be deported to Siberia. Fortunately, this son survived a ten-year sentence at forced labor and returned to Lithuania. After her husband Antanas died in1940, Magdalena had continued to live for some time on the farm with her son Petras. However, the daughter-in-law was a difficult person, so Magdalena moved to the small town of Veiveriai to stay with her daughter Monika's family. She died there in 1965, at the age of 82, and is buried in the Veiveriai cemetery.

Magdalena was a skilled farmwife. She knew how to weave and to sew clothing for the family, to embroider and knit, to feed a large family with meager resources, to preserve food for the winter, to take care of the farm animals and the vegetable gardens. But she also loved to sing and knew many songs; she was an excellent storyteller. Kazys remembered his mother as energetic, hard working, cheerful, and sociable. However, she had no schooling — she had learned to read the prayer book but not to write. She dictated her letters to her daughter Monika.

The first letter after World War II that Kazys received from his mother is translated below. She wrote in response to a letter she had received from him. Since these were the years of guerilla warfare against the Russian occupation and thousands of Lithuanians were arrested and killed, or deported to Siberia, Magdalena had to be cautious in her letter. She gave few specifics: "We had to suffer a lot in this difficult time; it would be too hard to describe everything." She mentioned that the health of various family members was poor, and that many friends and relatives had died. She stated that Monika's lungs were failing, Indeed, Monika died later of tuberculosis. Without voicing criticism, she referred to the forced collectivization of the farms when she said that Monika's husband's family, the Atmanavičiai, had lost theirs. Although she mentioned a "sister-in-law" who can forward mail from Kazys in Germany to his family in Lithuania, I believe that this intermediary was none other than Zosė (Sofija), our mother Jadvyga's cousin. Zosė, who brought us out of Lithuania, ended up behind the Iron Curtain herself, when she married a Polish refugee and returned with him to Poland. At that time, it was easier for mail from the West to reach Poland and then be forwarded to Lithuania.

Magdalena's last letter to Kazys is a heart-breaking cry of farewell to a beloved son who was torn from her by the war and the Russian occupation.

My beloved son and daughter-in-law,

It's been a long time since we saw each other. I was overcome with joy to learn that you are well and alive. I had not imagined that you had survived. Wherever I went, I thought to myself that I would never know where your young bodies are buried. How painful for me that I raised so many dear children, and now they have scattered all over the world; and in my grey old age I cannot see them and cannot know where they are. So, my dear Kazys, we are still well and alive, although our family has lost poor dear Antanas. We have news that he died in Russia with his whole family. We had to suffer a lot in this difficult time; it would be too hard to describe everything. Our Joseph with his family is living in Kaunas, living in poor conditions. Vladas is living with his family in Lazdijai. Damutė lives 12 km outside of Marijampolė, in the village of Dambava, still doing the same work [Damutė's husband was a forester]; *up to now they are all well. Petras also lives in the same place* [as before] *and all are well.*

A big change occured in the Atmanavičius family [Monika's in-laws]; *their Antanas died suddenly on December 23, 1945. The Atmanavičius family no longer has a farm — it's now administered by an office of animal husbandry and poor Juozas* [Monika's husband] *is kept on as a worker.* [Magdalena means the Atmanavičius farm was collectivized.] *Juozas' father, old Atmanavičius, died this year on May 19. There are four in* [Monika's] *family: the two of them* [Monika and her husband Juozas], *their son, little Gintautas, and daughter Danguolė who is seven and a half months old. But dear Monika's health is poor. The doctor admits that her lungs are failing— she has suffered a lot. They are all dear to me I now live with them and my health is also not good.*

Vladas had come home to visit for St. Peter's Feast Day [June 29]. *He has lost weight and he complains that his daughters are weak; they are now in secondary school. Your uncle Jasius Baranauskas died already in May this year; all the Baranauskas relatives have died. We received a letter from America — your aunt* [Ieva] *has died; only her children wrote back. Who knows, dear Kazys, if I will live to see you again or not. I want so much to see you again; then it would be easier to die. Many of our friends are gone — so many changes occured during the last war. Juozas Ješkevičius died already two years ago and Mrs. Ješkevičienė is doing poorly. So that's the news here. When you get this letter, then send an answer to us through your sister-in-law, she will send it on to us, if you can't do it any other way. We will be waiting for an answer from you.*

Kisses to all of you. Your loving mother.
Goodbye, goodbye. I wish you all the best.

July 10, 1947

Last Letter from Kazys' Mother, Magdalena Baranauskienė, in Lithuania
Dictated to her daughter Monika in spring 1965
Sent to Savin Hill Avenue, Boston, MA

Dear Loved Ones,
I [Monika] *am writing this letter to you in the words of our beloved mother.*

We received your Easter greetings and I received your greetings to me for Mothers' Day as well. From my heart I thank you — you did not forget me up to the hour of my death. And now I am writing you my last letter — you will not receive any more words from me. I am struck down by a serious illness; I've been sick since Christmas, but since Easter I've been feeling very badly. On the Tuesday after Easter I went to the hospital where I stayed for three weeks, but it did not help at all, I only felt worse. Now I am lying in bed at home and do not get up to walk at all. I hurt all over — I don't know what kind of illness this is, since no medicine helps. I thought that I would still be able to enjoy this summer, to walk around as before, but it seems that I will have to leave everything — how sad and painful.

I was waiting eagerly for your little package, but it seems I will not live to see it. I ask you for one thing, dear son, — you took care of me all these years, take care of me also after death. Give offerings for Masses for my soul, since I will not need anything else. I would like so much to live longer and I am afraid of dying. I was enjoying this life at last, after all those troubles in the past. I have no more strength left, this illness has made me weary. It is hard for me and for those around me. Everyone comes to visit me and feels sorry for me; they bring me all kinds of things, but nothing helps. Only you, my dear son, do not visit me and that makes me sad. I don't want to eat at all, unless I force myself. My left arm is badly swollen. This sickness is hard in my old age — I suffer and I am a burden to others. But what can one do... it is God's will.

My dear son and daughter-in-law, I am grateful that you remembered me all my life, that you provided me with everything, and even now had planned to send me something. I was waiting for it [the package], *telling myself that perhaps I did not need anything, but still, I wanted the pleasure of holding these things in my hands. If you have already mailed it, dear Monika will get it — because of me she struggles night and day. So now I will finish saying my farewell to you. I kiss you warmly a thousand times my beloved Kazys, my daughter-in-law, and all the grandchildren. I will have to leave you this spring — I had not expected that. Don't forget me as long as you live. Once more, I say farewell my dear children, wherever you are, scattered around the world. My last word, goodbye. Hold your dear mother in your memory.*

In a follow-up letter, Monika announced that mother Magdalena had died on June 12, 1965. Her illness was diagnosed as lung cancer.

~~~~~~~~~~~~~~

Letter from Siberia from Kazys' Brother Petras Baranauskas
Written July 22, 1957, from the Abakan region
Sent to Savin Hill Avenue, Boston, MA

Petras (Peter), born in 1908, was four years older than Kazys, the closest brother in age but different in temperament. According to Kazys, Petras was rather impulsive and hot headed, but also clever — a man with will power and initiative. Arrested by the Soviets in May 1948, he was deported to the remote, mountainous Abakan region (Republic of Khakassia) in Siberia where he spent ten years in a forced labor camp cutting trees in the forests. Petras wrote the following letter in 1957, a year before his release and return to Lithuania. In order for the letter to pass the camp censors, Petras had to be very careful in what he said. Readers need to read between the lines to understand what he was really trying to convey. He used humor and irony to suggest opposite meanings for he could not say how bad life was in the camps. The deportees were essentially slaves, receiving barely enough food to stay alive, so his line about "cramming money into our pockets" must be understood as an attempt at black humor. Petras mentioned that it took 18 days for him to reach Siberia by train; however, he does not say that the prisoners were transported in cattle wagons. His comment that those deportees who had "bad hearts" have gone to other places may be understood as a metaphor — death was the usual way out of the Gulags. People perished from starvation, exhaustion, and disease. Weather is a safe topic, so Petras spent a good portion of his letter talking about it, although he realized that Kazys probably knew all this. Sadly, when he finally returned to Lithuania, he found his wife living with another man. He divorced her and married again. Petras was an optimistic, energetic man who remained unbroken in spirit after ten brutal years in Siberia. He died in Kaunas in 1993.

My dear friend Kazimieras,

I greet you and your dear family from far-away Siberia. You write to me from one side of the globe, I write to you from the other side of the globe, and I say to you thank you, thank you again and again for your letter — that you took the time to write and did not forget me living in far-away Siberia. I live in the midst of impenetrable forests — their dimensions can't be measured; where even now snow covers the mountaintops, still not melted; where the rivers roar with rushing waters. And in this immense Siberian forest, I am cutting trees left and right, a meter or more in breadth. I scare the bears down from the trees. And the bears run away from me, other animals too — hawks, marals [red deer]; in a word, these forests are interesting. This region is devilishly mountainous. The cliffs are so steep that it frightens me to look down. But people do live here, some hunt, others fish.

The trees are taken to the river and floated down. The name of the river is Abakan. The river carries the logs to the city of Abakan. And that's how we live, cramming money into our pockets with both hands. From us to the city of Abakan is a distance of about 300 km [about 200 miles]. Kazimieras, take a look at a map and you will find the city of Abakan and the river. To reach us from the city of Abakan, one must travel upriver [southwest into the Sayan Mountains]. The Abakan River flows into the Yenisei River.

Then you asked about our weather. Well, it's similar to Lithuania. But of course, those who have bad hearts find it difficult here because this climate is very hard. I live about 3 km higher [at an elevation of about 9,000 feet] than the village of our birth and about 8,000 km [5,000 miles] from it. From our village I spent about 18 days on a train to distant Siberia. I arrived in May [he probably means June]1948; I left home on the 22 of May. Most of those whose hearts are bad have already left for other places. And then the winters are cold but calm, not much wind; temperatures -40 to -50 degrees C [-40 to -58 F] but the air is dry. The winters are healthier than in Lithuania. There's a lot of snow, to the depth of about 1meter 40 centimeters [4.5 feet]. But that snow is light like ashes, not as heavy as in Lithuania. And the summers too are similar to Lithuania, just hotter. Like back home, potatoes grow here, people raise pigs and cows. Here where I live there are about 15 Lithuanian families. There used to be more, but they left for other places.

So Kazimieras, you say that you can send medicine — send me something for my heart, to strengthen it, and for rheumatism. I too feel that my heart is getting weaker.

Further from me, about 50 km [30 miles] away, live other small groups of Lithuanians; the post office too is about 50 km away. In summer mail is delivered on horseback or by motor boat on the river. In winter, when the river freezes over, they deliver with horse and sleigh. In a word, we are living alright.

You ask me when I will come home. I just don't get around to it; I intend to, but I am amazed how quickly time passes. I should go home, since I left my family at home. I don't have a good photo of myself to send you, so just for now I'm sending you this one. Perhaps in the future I'll send you a better one — there's no photographer here; the closest lives 50 km away. So Kazimieras, try to *send me your photographs of the whole family, including photos of your children and your wife. I wonder how you all look; I may not recognize you any more. So then, what more can I write about the weather in Siberia? You went to school and you know yourself. Just try to send me the medicine I requested. Otherwise, I don't miss anything — I'm living alright, waiting for letters from you. I'm missing everyone, everyone.*

Goodbye,
Petras, your brother
July 22, 1957

12/18

Made in the USA
Columbia, SC
16 November 2018